D0645497

Florida
Wne Country
Guide to Northern Wineries

Pamela Watson

Woodhaven Publishing Shallotte, North Carolina

Published by:
Woodhaven Publishing
126 Wildwood Street, NW
Shallotte, North Carolina 28470

ISBN 978-0-9667116-4-6
Library of Congress Control Number: 2017913360

All care has been taken to assure that the information contained in this book, including addresses, telephone numbers, web sites, e-mail addresses, and all content, is complete and correct. However, these items sometimes change faster than it is possible to keep up with them. The author and publisher assume no responsibility for errors, inaccuracies, omissions, changes, or inconsistencies. Any slights of people, places, or organizations are purely unintentional.

The article concerning wine and health is not an endorsement for drinking wine or any other alcoholic beverage. Its purpose is to introduce some of the research being done into the relationship of wine and heart, and other diseases. For further readings on the subject, please refer to the links provided in the article. Consult your doctor before making any changes regarding your lifestyle and the consumption of alcohol.

Note: No one should consume alcohol and operate motor vehicles or machinery. It is not only unsafe, it is unlawful. Likewise, people with problematic drinking in their family histories should avoid alcohol. Be safe, be smart. Don't drink and drive.

Photo Credits
All photos are by Pamela Watson, except as designated below, and may not be used without written permission

Photo on page 83 courtesy of Katya Vineyards
Photo on page 89 courtesy of The Corkscrew Winery
Photo on page 123 courtesy of Dr. Violeta M. Tsolova, FAMU Viticulture Center
Photos on pages 165, 167, and 169, courtesy of Bethany Wilson and De Luna Winery

Front cover and author photos by Gillian Claire Photography, Myrtle Beach, South Carolina, www.gillianclaire.com

For my wonderful husband, Nick.
He cooks, I pour the wine.
It's a perfect partnership.

Acknowledgements

A book of any kind is always a collaborative effort. No author is ever out there on his or her own, I certainly am not. Without the assistance, advice, and suggestions of many wonderful people, this book could never have been written.

First, a huge THANK YOU goes to the winemakers and winery owners who took time to talk with me about their businesses, how they got started, and why they do what they do. They are an amazing group of people who spend their lives creating liquid art for the rest of us to enjoy.

Thanks also to Jeanne Burgess and Lakeridge Winery in Clermont, Florida for some valuable historical background information, to Dr. Violeta Tsolova, Professor of Viticulture and Developmental Biology at Florida A&M University for lots of grape facts and information, and to the Florida Department of Agriculture for their listings of wineries and information about the Florida grape and wine industry.

A big thank you also goes to J. R. Newbold and the wonderful members of the Florida Wine and Grape Growers' Association who encouraged me to write this book and who dedicate their time and talents to furthering the mission of growing grapes and making wine.

I owe a debt of gratitude to the folks at the Chambers of Commerce, Tourist Development Councils, and Convention and Visitors' Bureaus who provided me with information about their towns and counties, and who gave me some super ideas for places to eat, stay, and shop while you're in their areas.

Thanks too, to Sarah Aschliman of Island Grove Wine Company who is working on a Gainesville-area wine and brew trail. Her ideas were an inspiration to me and I appreciate our conversations and creative time.

Special thanks go to Sue and Max Elliott of the Florida Wine and Grape Growers' Association, who are themselves grape growers, winemakers, and teachers of the vine. Sue found a copy of my *Northwest Florida Wine Tour*, tracked me down in North Carolina and invited me to speak about wine trails at the FWGGA annual conference. They encouraged me to get back to work on this book and have kept me on track, for which I'm very grateful.

And finally, to my wonderful husband Nick, I give a big kiss and a hug for tolerating me spending many days on the road doing interviews, and countless hours wordsmithing on the computer. Of his many talents, his ability to know just when to tap on my office door and hand me a glass of wine at the end of the day is uncanny.

Table of Contents

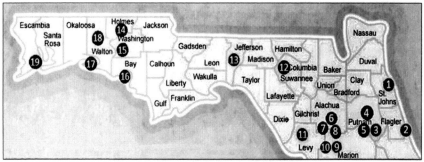

Map adapted from the Florida Department of Agriculture

North Florida Wineries

1 – San Sebastian Winery, *St. Augustine*

2 – Flagler Beachfront Winery, *Flagler Beach*

3 – Log Cabin Farm Vineyard and Winery, *Satsuma*

4 – Tangled Oaks Vineyard and Winery, *Grandin*

5 – Royal Manor Winery, *Interlachen*

6 - Bluefield Estate Winery, *Windsor*

7 – Micanopy Winery, *Micanopy*

8 – Island Grove Wine Company, *Island Grove*

9 – Katya Vineyards - *Ocala*

10 – The Corkscrew Winery - *Ocala*

11 - Dakotah Vineyards & Winery, *Chiefland*

12 – Mitillini Vineyards, *Live Oak*

13 – Monticello Vineyards & Winery, *Monticello*

Northwest Florida Wineries

14– Old Oaks Vineyard, *Bonifay*

15 – Three Oaks Winery, *Vernon*

16 – Panama City Beach Winery, *Panama City Beach*

17 – Emerald Coast Wine Cellars, *Miramar Beach*

18 – Chautauqua Vineyards & Winery, *DeFuniak Springs*

19 – De Luna Winery, *Pensacola*

"Most works of art,
like most wines,
ought to be consumed
in the district of their fabrication."

- Rebecca West (1892–1983)
British author

Foreword from the FWGGA

The official founding date of the Florida Grape Growers' Association (FGGA) is 1923, but historical records indicate that efforts to form the organization began far earlier, perhaps as early as 1914. No matter the date, the purpose of the FGGA was then, and still is, to serve farmers and hobbyists interested in growing grapes in Florida.

Created as a nonprofit corporation, the FGGA was instrumental in sponsoring research at the University of Florida to develop grape varieties adapted to Florida's growing conditions. Significantly, in 1978, the FGGA also encouraged the Florida Legislature to establish the Center for Viticulture and Small Fruit Research at Florida A&M University in Tallahassee (see page 122).

The Association continues to sponsor viticulture research, and works collectively with a variety of business and government entities to develop awareness about Florida wine and the unique qualities and health benefits of Florida grapes. It provides extensive information to those interested in making wine, growing Florida grapes, and producing grape products.

To recognize both commercial and hobbyist winemakers, and those who make wine from products other than grapes, the FGGA renamed itself in 2015 and became the Florida Wine and Grape Growers' Association (FWGGA). The organization continues to provide its members with access to university research, information on how to make wine and grow grapes, marketing ideas, contests and competitions, and networking opportunities through its website, various workshops, and the annual conference in January.

The website www.fwgga.org provides a means for interaction and resource sharing among members. The FWGGA Facebook page encourages information sharing and social interaction. Our online presence is something our founders never dreamed of, but it is essential for communication in the digital age.

As we approach our first 100 years as an organization, the Florida Wine and Grape Growers' Association is proud of the role we have played in the history and growth of Florida's grape and wine industry. This book is a natural extension of the FWGGA grape and wine education efforts, and we are happy to have played a part in encouraging its creation. Read the book, visit the wineries, and talk with the growers and winemakers. Most of all try Florida wine. You'll be glad you did.

Welcome to Wine Country
How to use this book

When I first wrote about the wine industry of the Carolinas back in the last century ("Carolina Wine Country The Complete Guide,"©1999), state wines were only just beginning to make themselves known. At that time, the state of Florida had six commercial wineries; San Sebastian Winery in St. Augustine, Lakeridge Winery and Vineyards in Clermont, Eden Winery in Alva, Dakotah Winery in Chiefland, Florida Orange Grove, Inc. & Winery in St. Petersburg, and Chautauqua Vineyards & Winery in DeFuniak Springs. My, how things have changed!

As of this writing, Florida has over 43 wineries, nearly half of them in North Florida. Some of these are vineyards with a winery and some are tasting rooms with a wine fermentation or processing component. All of them produce unique wines from Florida-grown fruits, but they may also use fruits and juices brought in from other locations. (For the list of Central and South Florida wineries, see the next to last page of this book.)

The Florida Department of Agriculture and Consumer Services has created an agritourism designation called "Certified Florida Farm Winery." There are currently 30 of these throughout the state, 13 of them in North Florida. This certification has nothing to do with the type or quality of wine made, but rather the amount, and a few other factors. Certified wineries are required to produce and sell less than 250,000 gallons of wine per year, 60% of which must be made from Florida agricultural products. They must maintain a minimum of 5 acres of vineyards in Florida, and be open to the public for tours, tastings, and sales at least 30 hours a week.

Although I've been drinking wine far longer than I've been writing about it, I've always found that wine is a fun subject, and touring wineries is a fun activity. When I wrote *Carolina Wine Country*, my children were high school age. I remember dropping them off at school one morning and telling them they needed to hitch a ride home with a friend because I was visiting a winery that day. They groaned as teenagers do, so I said, "Hey, how many kids do you know who have a mom who drinks wine for a living?" The groan changed to eye rolling. Then, over the summer, one of them went with me on interviews (getting to drive the car was a great incentive) and she found out that what I really did was record the stories of how and why people choose to grow grapes and make wine. It's a passion that all winemakers and vineyard owners share no matter what their background.

When I started working on this *Florida Wine Country Guide to Northern Wineries*, I decided to include all the North and Northwest Florida commercial wineries together. Doing so makes for a long stretch of driving across the Panhandle, but it also allows you to experience the 500-year history of Florida winemaking in the region where it has taken place.

The tour begins and ends in two of the oldest cities in America, St. Augustine and Pensacola. Traveling from the Atlantic Ocean to the Gulf of Mexico, you'll explore the modern-day vineyards and wineries that grew from 16th Century beginnings, meet the winemakers, and see why Florida wine is the oldest new wine in the country.

In my research and travels, I met some of the most fascinating people, people you'll meet in these pages and when you visit their wineries. They come from varied backgrounds and interests, but the love of growing grapes and making wine are their common goals. Don't miss the chance to talk with them about how and why they do what they do.

So, who can use this book? Well, families, couples, singles, wine lovers, and people who have never tasted wine for a start. It is for armchair travelers, seasoned travelers, and people who want to go somewhere different for a Saturday outing. Don't be afraid to bring the children, bring a picnic, bring the camera. Explore!

One thing to keep in mind is that Florida is one of those states that straddles two time zones, so you'll want to be sure and make note of winery opening times. All the wineries east of and including Monticello Vineyards & Winery are in the Eastern Time Zone. The six wineries west of Monticello are in the Central Time Zone, and I've indicated that on the opening times of the wineries and the local attractions and businesses. You'll cross the time zone just west of Tallahassee and you'll gain an hour in your day, which means more time for wine.

The book also includes state parks and historic sites, unique shopping, attractions, and fun places to eat near each winery. Depending on the time available, you can create a day trip, a weekend getaway or a whole vacation around wine tasting.

Now, that's my kind of road trip.

Pamela Watson
Shallotte, North Carolina

Muscadine grapes are native to the Southeastern United States and were the first grapes cultivated by European settlers.

Florida Grapes and Wine ~ A Brief History

It may surprise the casual traveler to learn that wine has been produced in Florida since the first European settlers put out their welcome mats. In fact, Florida was the first place in the New World where wine was produced commercially.

Two years before William Shakespeare was born in England, French Huguenots settled in Florida in an area near the St. Johns River and discovered wild grapes growing in abundance. These Muscadine grapes were like nothing the French had ever seen. They were *Vitis rotundifolia*, round grapes that grew in clusters not bunches. Being native to the southern states, they were not prone to diseases like the European varieties, *Vitis vinifera*, which couldn't tolerate the Florida climate. What's more, these native grapes were found to be perfect for winemaking.

Through the years, some notable historic figures were Muscadine wine aficionados. Thomas Jefferson loved wines made from the "Scuppernong," a whitish-bronze colored grape, and tried to cultivate it at his home in Monticello. Unfortunately for Jefferson, Muscadine grapes reach their maximum growing latitude in southern

Virginia and the climate of the Virginia foothills was too cold for cultivation. Today, however, there is a Muscadine vineyard and winery in Monticello – Monticello, FLORIDA, that is – and it is included in this guidebook. Jefferson would have been proud.

Evidence of planted grapevine arbors from around the 1640s has been found at the ruins of San Luis Mission in what is now Tallahassee. In 1837, a German traveler named Bromme mentioned seeing grapes growing in both Pensacola and Tallahassee.

In the early 1800s, the Marquis de Lafayette of Revolutionary War fame was given a large land grant near present day Tallahassee by the newly minted U.S. government. He commissioned vineyards to be grown there "for the purpose of making wines." It is not known if Lafayette ever visited these vineyards or how much wine, if any, was produced. What is known is that the idea of growing grapes in Florida is an old one, and that just prior to Prohibition in the 1920s, Florida had more than 4000 acres of vineyards.

In 1923, a grape research and breeding program was established at the University of Florida which, over the years, has resulted in the development of numerous disease resistant grape varieties suited to Florida's soil and climate. They are also suited to winemaking and produce a variety of wines from light and fruity to full-bodied with abundant fruit flavor.

Until recently, the commercial wine industry in Florida was slow to grow. In the past five or ten years, professional winemakers from the north have moved into the state, and a number of amateurs have taken the leap of faith and opened commercial wineries. Research at Florida A&M University and the University of Florida continues to help boost the growth of wineries in Florida and in states like North Carolina and Virginia.

As you drive along the Florida back roads, keep an eye out for grapevines, particularly in the backyards of some of the old homesteads. In the 19th and early 20th centuries, it was common to grow Muscadine grapes and families enjoyed fresh fruit, jams, pies, and a jug to two of wine throughout the year. Don't be surprised to see massive vines that are over 100 years old. Muscadine vines are hearty and long-living.

For more Florida grape history, see
http://mrec.ifas.ufl.edu/grapes/history

Scuppernong grapes grow in clusters

The Mighty Muscadine

Over the centuries, wine has been recommended for the treatment of iron deficiency anemia ("A little wine will build up your blood."), sleep disorders ("A glass of wine before bedtime will help you sleep better."), and stress ("Have a glass of sherry, dear. It will calm your nerves."). It has been prescribed for upset stomachs, to aid digestion, and to help increase the absorption of minerals and nutrients. Much of this advice has been attributed to "old wives' tales" or folk medicines, but in the past 20 years or so, some scientific studies have found that a glass of wine each day with your meal reduces the risk of heart attack and other diseases. Is it possible then that wine truly is a miracle elixir for good health?

When most people think of the wine in their glass, they think of European grapes, *Vitis vinifera,* also called bunch grapes. This variety includes Riesling, Chardonnay, Merlot, Pinot Noir and others. The variety of grapes native to America, *Vitis rotundifolia* or round grapes, are often called cluster grapes because of the way they grow in clusters rather than bunches. These are Muscadine grapes and include, among others, the varieties Carlos (sometimes called Scuppernong), Magnolia, Noble, Doreen, and Nesbitt, which range in coloring from white to bronze to black. They are generally larger than bunch grapes and grow to about an inch or more in diameter, or as the old-timers used to say, about as big as a hog's eye.

In the early 1990s, studies began on the health benefits of drinking wine because of the so-called French Paradox. It was a known fact that the French developed coronary heart disease at less than half the rate of Americans despite a diet high in fat, relatively little exercise, and heavy smoking habits. The difference was that the French drink wine with their meals and wine was found to contain an antioxidant called Resveratrol, a substance that is associated with reduced coronary heart disease, lower cholesterol levels, and anticarcinogenic properties, active against all stages of cancer. At first only European grape varietals were tested, then in the mid-1990s scientists began to look at the Muscadine grape. What they found was extraordinary.

The studies showed that Muscadine grapes have the highest concentration of Resveratrol, their skins, seeds and pulp acting as a leading food source for fighting cancer. They are also the only grapes that contain Resveratrol in the seed. Muscadines are fat free, high in fiber, and high in ellagic acid, a substance which has demonstrated anticarcinogenic properties in the lungs, colon, and liver of laboratory mice.

It is important to note that the health benefits of drinking Muscadine wine, or any other wine, are maximized with one to three glasses of wine **with a meal**. Drinking more than three glasses increases health risks. However, drinking with dinner assures that the protective effects are strongest in the evening when fats from the meal circulate through the bloodstream, and carry over to the next morning when most heart attacks occur.

However, there is good news for non-wine drinkers. Besides wine, Muscadines are now marketed as juice, jellies, jams, preserves, syrups, dessert toppings, and as dietary supplements, utilizing the seeds, skins, and stems to produce Muscadine tablets. Then too, there's always the original way to consume the fruit and that's to eat it right off the vine.

Now, that's a mighty versatile grape.

Find more wine and health information in these online articles:

Broustet, J.P., "Wine and Health," Heart and Education in Heart, 1999
http://heart.bmj.com/content/81/5/459.extract

Percival Susan S., Sims Charles A., Talcott Stephen T., "Immune Benefits of Consuming Red Muscadine Wine", September 2002- Febryary 2017, University of Florida, Institute of Food and Agricultural Sciences (IFAS) Extension
http://edis.ifas.ufl.edu/pdffiles/FS/FS08500.pdf

"The Health Benefits of Muscadine Grapes, Wines and Nutraceuticals," M. D. News, June 2008
www.nccommerce.com/Portals/10/Documents/MD%20News%20June%202008.pdf

"Red wine and resveratrol: Good for your heart?" Mayo Foundation for Medical Education and Research (MFMER)
http://www.mayoclinic.org/diseases-conditions/heart-disease/in-depth/red-wine/ART-20048281

Baby Muscadine Grapes

"What wond'rous life is this I lead!
Ripe apples drop about my head;
The luscious clusters of the vine
Upon my mouth do crush their wine..."

- Andrew Marvell, 1621-1678
English Poet

San Sebastian Winery

157 King Street
St. Augustine, Florida 32084
904-826-1594
1-888-352-9463
www.sansebastianwinery.com

Hours: Monday – Saturday, 10:00 a.m. to 6:00 p.m.
Sunday, 11:00 a.m. to 6:00 p.m.
Wine Tasting: Free

Long before English poet Andrew Marvell was born, French Huguenots and Spanish monks were making wine in Florida. Today, like those pioneers who came before them, the winemakers at San Sebastian Winery carry on a tradition that is over 450 years old. Using native Muscadine grapes, and more recently developed Florida hybrids, they craft their wines using age-old methods for today's wine lovers. The result is wines made for food and fun.

Established in 1996, San Sebastian Winery is owned and operated by the Cox family, long time grape growers, winemakers, and pioneers in the Florida grape and wine industry. San Sebastian is also a sister to Lakeridge Winery & Vineyards in Clermont, Florida where the grapes for both wineries are grown and crushed.

Overlooking the San Sebastian River, from which the winery gets its name, and just steps away from the downtown historic district of St. Augustine, San Sebastian Winery's location is both symbolic of Florida wine history and the perfect spot for wine tasting.

The winery comprises 18,000 square feet, one third of which is a circa 1923 Florida East Coast Railway building. San Sebastian's warehouse has a 40,000-gallon wine storage capacity that includes both 5000-gallon stainless steel tanks and 52-gallon oak barrels. The winery also features a retail shop and tasting room, another tasting room for overflow and private groups, and a rooftop wine bar called The Cellar Upstairs where local musicians perform on the weekends.

A visit to San Sebastian Winery can take a few minutes to a couple of hours depending on how long you browse, shop, and taste. Although there are no vineyards to see, the rooftop view is fabulous, and you should definitely take the free wine tour.

Beginning and ending in the retail shop, the tour takes about 45 minutes and includes an introductory video on Florida wine history. Knowledgeable guides offer insights on grape cultivation and wine production and they are happy to answer your questions. You'll see production facilities where they bottle the port and cream sherry, storage tanks and barrels where they age the port, and there are a number of historical wine production artifacts along the way.

The tasting bar at San Sebastian Winery is made from old barrels.

Tours are offered daily starting at 10:00 a.m. (11:00 a.m. on Sunday) and run about every 20 minutes with the last tour leaving at 5:00 p.m.

However, the best part is the tasting. Your guide will walk you through the intricacies of several wines, what grapes are used, how they're made, and what foods are best to pair them with. He or she will also give you some fun ideas like putting frozen fruit in your wine to keep it cool, and you can ask to try something not on the tasting list, as long as it's in stock.

On Fridays, Saturdays, and Sundays San Sebastian's rooftop venue, The Cellar Upstairs, rocks the winery with live music and wines and beers served by the glass. Lunch is available starting at 11:30 a.m. with a menu that includes appetizers, salads, sandwiches, and meat and cheese platters. The Cellar Upstairs is open Friday and Saturday from 11:30 a.m. to 11:00 p.m. and Sunday from 11:30 a.m. to 6:00 p.m.

Before you leave, be sure to check out the retail store for take-home items and gifts. Of course, there's wine, so you'll want to add several bottles of your favorite to your cart, but you'll also find unique glassware, cookbooks, tee-shirts, wine storage and gadgets, jams and jellies, and dips, dressings, and desserts.

San Sebastian's tag line is "Enjoy a taste of history." With America's first city just around the corner, you can certainly do that.

Tasting San Sebastian Winery wines is the best part.

San Sebastian Winery

Directions

San Sebastian Winery is located in St. Augustine, Florida. From Interstate 95 going north, take exit 311 and head east on Highway 207 to U.S. Highway 1. Turn left onto U.S. 1 and go to West King Street. Turn right o nto West King Street. The winery is on your right after you cross the river.

From Interstate 95 South, take exit 318 and go east on Highway 16 until you reach U.S. 1. Turn right onto U.S. 1 and go to West King Street. Turn left onto West King Street. The winery is on your right after you cross the river.

San Sebastian Winery Wine List

Vintners Red – intense fruit flavor derived from the Noble variety of the Native Muscadine grape, serve slightly chilled as a complement to any pasta dish or for just sipping and relaxing

Vintners White – made from native Muscadine grapes, full bodied, slightly sweet, and with fruity character, enjoy this wine with any highly flavored meal or with fruits and cheeses

Reserva – a dry white wine with the best characteristics of several of Florida's Hybrid Bunch grapes that complements fish and poultry dishes, or for just sipping and relaxing

Rosa – made from native Florida Muscadine grapes. light, refreshing, and balanced with a hint of sweetness and a delicate fruity character that complements a variety of foods or for just sipping on a warm afternoon

Blanc du Bois – this richly flavored white wine with overtones of pear and melon and an intense fruit flavor goes well with strong cheeses, fish and chicken dishes, as well as spicy Asian cuisine

Blanc De Fleur – a sparkling wine with a hint of fruit and sweetness and tiny bubbles created in the traditional *Methode Champenoise*

Castillo Red – a dry red with a deep burgundy color, a hint of oak, and light on the tannins that goes well with meats or richer foods

Cream Sherry – a full bodied and sweet cream sherry with a rich amber color and nutty flavor that enhances the flavor of any dessert

Port – traditional aging in oak barrels adds to the character and flavor of this rich and fruity port dessert wine, with flavors of sweet raisins, currants, cherries, and spice

Also available are Chardonnay and Cabernet Sauvignon.

Castillo de San Marcos in St. Augustine

While you're here...

St. Augustine is the oldest city in America, but that doesn't mean it's a dry museum filled with dusty old relics. This historic city is alive with lots to see and do. Explore the downtown historic district, the old Spanish village, and Castillo de San Marcos. Browse an extensive collection of artworks at the Lightner Museum, walk in the footsteps of Martin Luther King, and see why Henry Flagler is Florida's most prominent pioneer. Then kick back with a cocktail and dinner at some of the area's top restaurants. There's enough to keep you busy for days, so here are a few suggestions to get you started.

Area Information
St. Augustine Visitor Information Center
10 S. Castillo Drive
St. Augustine, Florida 32084
904-825-1000   - www.visitstaugustine.com
Open daily 8:30 a.m. to 5:30 p.m.

Attractions
Lightner Museum
75 King Street
St. Augustine, Florida 32084
904-824-2874
www.lightnermuseum.org
Open daily except Christmas Day, 9:00 a.m. to 5:00 p.m.
Admission: $10 adults, $5 children 12 to 18, children under 12 free
Three floors of art, furniture, and collectibles from around the world

Castillo de San Marcos

1 S. Castillo Drive
St. Augustine, Florida 32084
904-829-6506
www.nps.gov/casa
Open daily except Thanksgiving Day and Christmas Day, 8:45 a.m. to 5:15 p.m.
Admission: $10 adults 16 and older, children 15 and under free
This 17th Century Spanish fort and National Monument is the oldest masonry fortress in the United States.

Ponce de Leon's Fountain of Youth Archaeological Park

11 Magnolia Avenue
St. Augustine, Florida 32084
904-829-3168
www.fountainofyouthflorida.com
Open daily 9:00 a.m. to 6:00 p.m.
Admission: $14 adults 13 and older, $13 seniors 60+, $8 children ages 6 to 12, children under 6 free
Original 1565 location of the St. Augustine settlement, includes 15 acres of gardens, archaeological sites, interpreters, and living history

St. Augustine Alligator Farm Zoological Park

999 Anastasia Boulevard
St. Augustine, Florida 32080
904-824-3337
www.alligatorfarm.com
Open daily 9:00 a.m. to 5:00 p.m.
Admission: $24.99 adults 12 and older, $13.99 children ages 3 to 11
Founded in 1893, and one of the oldest zoos in the country, home to crocodiles, alligators, other reptiles, monkeys, and small mammals

St. Augustine Lighthouse & Maritime Museum

81 Lighthouse Avenue
St. Augustine, Florida 32080
904-829-0745
www.staugustinelighthouse.com
Open daily 9:00 a.m. to 6:00 p.m.
Admission: $12.95 adults 13 and older, $10.95 seniors 60+ and children 12 and under (must be 44 inches tall to climb)
Climb to the top of this 1874 lighthouse for a fantastic view. 219 steps

Bed & Breakfast (there are dozens but here are two of my favorites)
Casa de Solana Bed and Breakfast
21 Aviles Street
St. Augustine, Florida 32084
904-824-3555 - www.casadesolana.com

Casablanca Inn on the Bay
24 Avenida Menendez
St. Augustine, Florida 32084
904-829-0928 or 1-800-826-2626 (toll free)
www.casablancainn.com

Fun Eats
Columbia Restaurant
98 St. George Street
St. Augustine, Florida 32084
904-824-3341
www.columbiarestaurant.com
Authentic Spanish food for over 110 years

Cafe Alcazar
25 Granada Street (behind the Lightner Museum)
St. Augustine, Florida 32084
904-825-9948
www.thealcazarcafe.com
Soups, sandwiches, and seafood in an elegant setting

Shopping
Whetstone Chocolates
42 St. George Street & 139 King Street (factory tours)
St. Augustine, Florida 32084
904-825-1720 & 904-217-0275
www.whetstonechocolates.com
Chocolate - enough said!

Saint Augustine Art Glass
54 St. George Street
St. Augustine, Florida 32084
904-824-4916
www.saintaugustineartglass.com
Arts and crafts gallery with hand crafted stained glass made on site.

Flagler Beachfront Winery
Ken & Kelly Tarsitano
611 N. Oceanshore Boulevard
Flagler Beach, Florida 32136
386-693-4950
www.flaglerbeachfrontwinery.com

Hours: Sunday – Thursday, noon to 9:00 p.m.
Friday & Saturday, noon to 11:00 p.m.
Wine Tasting: 50 cents per wine sample

When you're a winemaker, you make wine. It's what you do. If you're Ken Tarsitano, you grow the grapes, make the wine, sell the wine, open a restaurant, teach grape growing and winemaking at Kent State University, move to Florida, open another winery – and that's just some of what you do.

To say the former Ohio State University Buckeye is a "do-er" is an understatement. In the early 1990s, armed with degrees in Psychology, Computer Science, Philosophy, Art and Photojournalism, the kid from the Cleveland suburbs set out to conquer the world. During his travels and adventures, Ken spent five years in advertising before going home to purchase his grandfather's dairy farm in 1996.

"I grew up on my grandparents' farm," Ken explains. "It gave me the best of all worlds."

At first Ken grew fruits, vegetables and nuts, but it was hard to make the investment pay off, so he soon turned to something his grandfather had taught him – making wine.

"If it bubbled, bottled, pickled or brewed, my grandfather did it in his home basement," says Ken.

His academic nature immediately led him to Ohio State University where he learned to grow grapes at OSU's grape and wine research center. It wasn't long before he was working there as a research assistant learning about organic viticulture practices.

In 1998, Ken planted his first grapevines and began making wine while continuing to work for the Ohio Agricultural Research and Development Center in nearby Kingsville. In 2000, Ken opened Tarsitano Winery & Vineyard, not far from the windswept shores of Lake Erie, and one of three wineries in the Conneaut, Ohio area.

Ken got his certification in organic grape production in 2001 and began lecturing and consulting on organic viticulture practices. But, things were moving faster than he had originally anticipated and in 2004, already some five years ahead of his business plan, he opened a restaurant at the winery.

"Forget your expectations," says Ken, remarking on how quickly life changes. "Embrace the adventure."

The adventure continued the following year when Ken married Kelly, a teacher with a dream of her own. Together they grew

Ken pours wine for customers at the tasting bar.

Living by the sea was Kelly's dream.

the grapes, made the wine and built their winery business. Kelly crafted delicious desserts for the restaurant while Ken taught viticulture and enology at Kent State. Then, after several years of working the vines and wines, Ken, Kelly and their three children moved to Florida.

"We had been visiting Florida for a long time. We had friends here and it was Kelly's dream to live at the beach. Flagler Beach was the perfect place for us. It's a small town and it has everything we love to do," says Ken.

With the idea of making wine by the sea, Ken and Kelly purchased the "little blue building," as their children dubbed it, a former Pizza Hut/Greek restaurant/real estate agency that overlooks the Atlantic Ocean and now houses both the wine shop and the fermentation room. All the wine production work is done here, but unfortunately there are no winery tours. The building is far too small for that and some of the production, such as grape crush, must be done outside, but you can view the stainless steel tanks and oak barrels through the glass partition while you sip some of Flagler Beachfront Winery's award winning wine.

The winery currently produces about 5,000 gallons of wine per year with a goal of 10,000 gallons in the near future. All the barrels and tanks are full of various wines that sell out as fast as Ken and Kelly can make them.

Ken says the part he plays is that of an artist rather than a manufacturer. He's a crafter, creating a one-of-a-kind artifact. He uses a variety of grapes; some grown on the farm in Ohio which he still owns and operates, some locally grown in Florida, and some purchased from vineyards across the country. And, just like an artist, he uses his knowledge and talent to create liquid art.

Ken himself favors full-bodied red wines, so the first wines he made were Cabernet Sauvignon and Merlot. His award-winning *Allure* is a Cabernet blend made from grapes brought in from across the country, and his Merlot and Syrah have also won awards.

But, knowing his customers like a variety, he offers everything from fruity white wines to Cabernet on tap (available only at the winery) to varietal blends. For those sizzling summer days, wine slushies hit the spot and locally grown grapes, blueberries, and watermelons make delicious wines to slush. The tag-line "Got Slushed" adorns caps and tee-shirts that are available for purchase.

"The fun thing about Florida is that we're not stuck on one grape, or even grapes at all," says Ken, indicating that wine can be made from anything.

Ken and Kelly still own and operate the vineyard and winery in Ohio, although they closed the restaurant when they moved to Flagler Beach. They maintain Flagler Beachfront Winery as a separate

The Little Blue Building by the Sea

business and the Florida winery buys some of its grapes from the Ohio vineyard.

Ken continues to lecture and consult, as well as to help the Florida wine industry to grow. He started the website FloridaWineTrail.org to help market other vineyards and wineries in the state. Additionally, he's a strong believer in buying locally and supporting local businesses, and buys as much Florida fruit for his wines as he can.

He also offers Florida craft beers on tap for those who prefer a brew. Breweries such as Orange Blossom in Orlando, Swamp Head in Gainesville, and Cigar City in Tampa are just a few of the featured beers and they are included on the daily drink specials menu along with wine slushies and wine cocktails. Tapas plates and boards that include cheeses, olives, prosciutto and pesto can be purchased and paired with the wines, and you can't beat the view.

After 20 years in the wine business, and a home and a winery by the sea, Ken and Kelly are living their dream. "Sometimes the dream finds you as much as you find the dream," Ken says.

Directions
From I-95, take Highway 100 east to Flagler Beach. Turn left on A1A and go six blocks. The winery is on your left and the ocean is on your right.

Flagler Beachfront Winery Wine List
All wines are subject to availability

Wines available by the bottle, by the glass, or on tap

Allure – a mysteriously attractive, berry driven medium body red blend

Merlot - rich, round, full body with warm tannins and a hint of vanilla

Red Zinfandel – rich raspberry, slightly sweet, hint of pepper with a soft dry finish

Petit Verdot - big, bold, jammy, dry red with ample tannins

Riptide - very smooth, fruity, sweet red Muscadine wine

Sweet Concord - sweet, very grapey, easy to drink

Organic Chardonnay – 2012 certified organic grapes from the vineyards in Ohio, a classic Chardonnay, dry, silky, and crisp with a smooth finish

Organic Pinot Gris - 2013 certified organic grapes from the vineyards in Ohio, a light, fruity, semi-dry wine

Elation - Uplifting blend of Pinot Gris, Riesling and Sauvignon Blanc, refreshing and lightly sweet

Organic Sauvignon Blanc – Dry, refreshing, medium body with tropical notes, lime and a light spicy finish. Made with grapes from the vineyards in Ohio.

Gewürztraminer – Interestingly spicy dry white wine with hints of dried fruit and honey. Made with Washington state grapes

Other Wines Sometimes Available

Riesling	Sauvignon Blanc	Dry Riesling
Pinot Gris	Traminette	Moscato
Pinot Noir	Cabernet Franc	Petite Syrah
Malbec		

Flagler Beach Pier

While you're here...

After you've sipped your slushy, nibbled some tapas, and purchased your Flagler Beachfront Winery wine to take home, you might want to check out the surroundings. Across the street is the beach, so go ahead and stick your toes in the sand and relax a while. A few blocks south is the Flagler Beach Pier where, for $1.50 per person you can walk to the end, watch anglers catch fish and enjoy the sea breeze. A few miles north on A1A are Marineland and Washington Oaks Gardens State Park. Both are worth the trip. To the south are Gamble Rogers Memorial State Recreation Area and historic Ormond Beach, which has a lot to do. Here are some more suggestions to help you explore.

Area Information
Flagler County Chamber of Commerce Visitor's Center
20 Airport Road, Suite C
Palm Coast, Florida 32164
386-437-0106   www.flaglerchamber.org
Open Monday – Friday, 9:00 a.m. to 5:00 p.m.

Attractions
Flagler Beach Historical Museum
207 S. Central Avenue
Flagler Beach, Florida 32136
386-517-2025
www.flaglerbeachmuseum.com
Open daily 10:00 a.m. to 4:00 p.m. – Admission Free
Small local history museum chock full of old photos and artifacts

Gamble Rogers Memorial State Recreation Area
3100 S. Oceanshore Boulevard
Flagler Beach, Florida 32136
386-517-2086
www.floridastateparks.org/park/Gamble-Rogers
Open daily 8:00 a.m. to sunset year-round
Admission: $5 per vehicle, camping fees additional
Swimming, hiking, RV and tent camping, birding, fishing and boating

Washington Oaks Gardens State Park
6400 N. Oceanshore Boulevard
Palm Coast, Florida 32137
386-446-6780
www.floridastateparks.org/park/Washington-Oaks
Open daily 8:00 a.m. to sunset year-round – Admission: $5 per vehicle
Formal gardens, nature trail, unique coquina rock formations

Bulow Plantation Ruins Historic State Park
3501 Old Kings Road
Flagler Beach, Florida 32136
386-517-2084
www.floridastateparks.org/park/Washington-Oaks
Open Thursday – Monday, 9:00 a.m. to 5:00 p.m.
Admission: $4 per vehicle
Ruins of a former sugar plantation, a sugar mill, a unique spring house,
several wells, the plantation house and slave cabins

Marineland Dolphin Adventure
9600 Ocean Shore Boulevard
St. Augustine, Florida 32080
904-471-1111 or 1-877-933-3402 (toll free)
www.marineland.net
Open daily year-round
9:00 a.m. to 4:30 p.m.
Admission: $14.95
ages 13 and older
$9.95 children
ages 3-12
$13.95 seniors 60+
Historic marine mammal
park and research center

Bed & Breakfast
The White Orchid Inn & Spa
1104 S. Oceanshore Boulevard
Flagler Beach, Florida 32136
386-439-4944 or 1-800-423-1477 (toll free)
www.whiteorchidinn.com

Island Cottage Oceanfront Inn & Spa
2316 S. Ocean Shore Boulevard
Flagler Beach, Florida 32136
386-439-0092 or 1-877-662-6232 (toll free)
www.islandcottagevillas.com

Fun Eats
Funky Pelican at the Flagler Beach Pier
215 Florida A1A
Flagler Beach, Florida 32136
386-439-0011
www.funkypelican.com
Breakfast through dinner; seafood, sandwiches, and salads on the Pier

Java Joint
2201 N. Ocean Shore Boulevard
Flagler Beach, Florida 32136
386-439-1013
www.javajointfb.com
Breakfast, brunch, vegetarian and vegan overlooking the ocean

Shopping
Ocean Art Gallery
206 Moody Boulevard (SR 100)
Flagler Beach, Florida 32136
386-693-4882   www.flagleroceanartgallery.com
Features local and national artists in various media

Down by the Sea Boutique & Art Gallery
208 S. 3rd Street
Flagler Beach, Florida 32136
386-439-2255
Old Florida style beachside boutique and art gallery features gifts
and local artwork

*With the growth of the grape
every nation elevates itself to a
higher grade of civilization.*

*- Friedrich Muench, 1799-1881
German-American winemaker,
author, and Missouri State Senator*

Log Cabin Farm, Vineyard & Winery

Kellie Thropp & Ruthann Thropp
376 County Road 309
Satsuma, Florida 32189
386-467-0000
www.logcabinfarmwinery.com

Hours: Friday, 11:00 a.m. to 5:00 p.m.
Saturday, 10:00 a.m. to 5:00 p.m.
Sunday, noon to 5:00 p.m.
Wine Tasting: $1 per wine

For three generations, the Thropp family has worked the land in Northeast Florida. Their 50 acres, once part of a large plantation in the historic community of Nashua, have grown citrus, housed chickens, nurtured the elegance and beauty of quarter horses, and most recently produced wine grapes.

Located just off U.S. Highway 17, about 14 miles south of Palatka, Log Cabin Farm, Vineyard & Winery is a family owned and operated Certified Florida Farm Winery. Today, the vineyard encompasses ten acres of mature Muscadine vines that supply high quality wine grapes to the growing Florida wine industry.

The Thropp's adventure began in 1949 when Ruthann's parents purchased the 50 acres and moved their family from the beaches of Miami to the interior wilds of "Old Florida." They cleared 10 acres, planted citrus, and raised chickens. Ruthann remembers growing up exploring the nearby woods and lakes with the historic St. Johns River practically in her backyard. She also remembers watching entranced as women pilots, members of Amelia Earhart's famous Ninety-Nines, would take off and land their airplanes in a nearby field, and she decided then and there that she wanted to be one of them.

She eventually got her pilot's license and met her husband Bob while the two were in the Navy during the Viet Nam War. After the war, they returned to the farm and Bob set up a dental practice in town while Ruthann became a counselor at the high school. They raised their children Bobby and Kellie on the farm, continuing to grow chickens and citrus, and adding quarter horses.

One day while on a trip south, Bob and Ruthann stopped in at Lakeridge Winery and enjoyed a wine tasting that would change their lives. As the guide talked about growing grapes and making wine, Bob said, "I could do that." Ruthann looked at him skeptically, but he insisted, so soon they were clearing land to plant vines.

"We put in our first acre in 1995 and then added another acre," says Ruthann. "We kept moving the horse pasture and adding more vines. We contracted to Lakeridge to sell them our grapes and in 1999 we harvested one ton."

Muscadine vines growing at Log Cabin Farm

That first harvest, and the ones after that, were picked by hand. Friends, family, neighbors, and a couple of hired hands all pitched in to get the grapes to market. Bob and Ruthann added more acreage and soon the annual harvest was up to six tons.

Then in 2004, disaster threatened. Charley, Frances, Ivan – it was a busy hurricane season for Florida. When hurricane Jeanne began to churn her way through the state in September, Bob and Ruthann knew they had to do something to get the grapes picked before the storm hit. So, they bought a harvester.

The purchase proved to be the right move in a lot of ways as their production increased and soon they were harvesting their own grapes and providing their harvesting services to other vineyards in the area.

In May 2009, Bob passed away, leaving Ruthann with the vineyard and no idea how to care for it. In the middle of the growing season, she found herself trying to learn how to grow grapes.

"I learned from my mistakes, and I made a lot of them," she says. "But, it was his dream and I wasn't about to relinquish it." She began by asking questions of anyone who knew about grape growing, from the local agricultural extensions to the experts at Florida A&M University.

Through trial and error, and a lot of hard work, Ruthann learned to propagate cuttings, prune vines, and to even try new varieties. Today, Log Cabin Farm grows native Florida Muscadine grapes Carlos, Noble, and Magnolia, and the Florida hybrid grape Blanc du Bois.

Meanwhile, Kellie, who lived nearby, had gotten hooked on winemaking. Helping her father plant, prune, and irrigate had given her an appreciation for the grapes. "It's where my roots are, pardon the pun," she says, smiling. She began making wine and entering it in amateur wine contests, winning a number of gold, silver, and bronze medals. In 2008, they decided to open the winery.

"We focus on growing quality wine grapes," says Kellie. "Our family philosophy is, without quality fruit, a quality wine cannot be produced and we really believe that."

Another focus is on the history of the farm and of the community. Log Cabin Farm hosts a couple of wine/history festivals during the year that include local authors and historians as well as artisans and musicians. They pride themselves in calling the area "Old Florida" and have researched local historical figures and events.

The interior of the wine tasting room reflects the history of the area as well as wine.

They are also active in an ongoing archaeological project, a coquina tabby house that is located on the property. Believed to be an old homestead built and occupied in the late 1800s by Emma Moody, the site has yielded glassware, pottery, and even wine bottles. Kellie says she hopes to create a historical destination with a hiking trail that would connect to the Putnam County Bartram Trail. "All the plants that Bartram wrote about can be found on our property," she says.

Along with wines for tasting and purchase, the small wine shop and tasting room features locally made Muscadine juices, sauces, jams, and jellies. There are also photographs of the farm over the years, and a collection of artifacts found on the property.

Wine tastings are $1 per wine sample and you can sample as many wines as you like. You can even bring a picnic lunch and spend a day in "Old Florida," purchase a bottle of wine, and then sit back and watch the vines grow.

Directions
From I-95, take State Road 100 west from Flagler Beach or State Road 207 from St. Augustine to US 17. Go south on US 17 to Satsuma, turn right onto County Road 309 and go about 2.9 miles. Log Cabin Farm is on your left.

Log Cabin Farm, Vineyard & Winery
Wine List
Wines may change without notice and are subject to availability

Black Gold – blackberry wine

Watermelon Wine – 'nuff said

Sinfully Noble – a premium Muscadine wine made from the Noble grape

Key Lime Wine – made with fresh Florida key limes

Sparkling Key Lime Reserve – a sparkling wine with a tropical feel

A reconstruction of the log cabin where the Thropp family once lived.
The original cabin burned in the 1950s.

Hiking trails abound in Putnam County.

While you're here...

Putnam County is located midway between Jacksonville and Orlando, with its eastern boundary lying about 20 miles inland from the coast. Timeless in nature, the county is largely rural and features vast areas of natural beauty and abundant wildlife, a perfect place to enjoy a variety of outdoor activities. There are several state parks and conservation areas, and the northeast corner of the Ocala National Forest is also here. The St. Johns River winds its way north through the east side of the county lending itself to boating, fishing, kayaking, and other water sports. The area really is a sportsperson's paradise.

Area Information
Putnam County Chamber of Commerce
1100 Reid Street
Palatka, Florida 32177
386-328-1503   - www.putnamcountychamber.com

Attractions
Dunns Creek State Park
320 Sisco Road
Pomona Park, Florida 32181
386-329-3721
www.floridastateparks.org/park/Dunns-Creek
Open daily 8:00 a.m. to sunset
Admission: $5.00 per vehicle
6200 acres with 4 miles of biking and hiking trails, picnic areas, wildlife viewing, kayaking and paddling

Murphy Creek Conservation Area

From U.S. 17 in Satsuma, turn west on County Road 309B (East Buffalo Road). There is a parking area approximately one-half mile on the north side of the road. Murphy Island north of the creek has about six miles of hiking trails. Access to Murphy Island is by boat only, either from the creek or the St. Johns River.

Bureau of Land Resources, 386-329-4404

Welaka State Forest Headquarters

County Road 309 just south of Welaka
Welaka, Florida 32193
386-467-2388

Over 2200 acres of hiking, horseback trails, and wildlife viewing. The 2-mile long Mud Spring Trail starts at the trailhead directly across from the forest headquarters. The John's Landing Trail is 3 to 4 miles long and is located at the fire tower site one mile south of the headquarters.

Welaka National Fish Hatchery and Aquarium

County Road 309
Welaka, Florida 32193
386-467-2374   www.fws.gov/welaka
Open daily 7:00 a.m. to 4:00 p.m. - Admission Free
Operated by the U.S. Department of Interior, the aquarium has reptiles and 22 tanks containing specimens of about 15 species of native freshwater fish.

Fort Gates Ferry
From County Road 309 go west on Mount Royal Avenue, then turn
right on Fort Gates Ferry Road (dirt road) and go .9 miles to the river
386-467-2411
Operates from 7:00 a.m. to 5:30 p.m. daily, except Tuesday – call ahead
to make sure the ferry is running
Fare: $9 per car
Since 1853, the oldest operating ferry in Florida shuttles passengers
and automobiles between Welaka and Ocala National Forest.

Lodging
Welaka Lodge & Resort
1001 Front Street
Welaka, Florida 32193
Channel Marker 50, Welaka
386-467-7171
www.welakalodge.com

Andersen's Lodge
10 Boston Street
Welaka, Florida 32193
386-467-2707
www.andersenslodge.com

Fun Eats
Shrimp R Us More
765 3rd Avenue
Welaka, Florida 32193
386-467-7111
www.shrimprusandmore.com
Sandwiches, seafood, steaks, and salad, serving breakfast, lunch, and
dinner

Hawg Wash BBQ Joint
114 S. 3rd Street
Palatka, Florida 32177 (formerly in Welaka)
386-524-4036
www.hawgwashbbqjoint.com
Sandwiches, burgers, plates, and barbecue by the pound

Tangled Oaks Vineyard & Winery

Dave DaCasto Family
1317 State Road 100
Grandin, Florida 32138
386-659-1707
www.tangledoaksvineyard.com

Hours: Tuesday – Friday, noon to 6:00 p.m.
Saturday, 10:00 a.m. to 6:00 p.m.
Wine Tasting: Free

D ave DaCasto didn't set out to be a winemaker. For 30 years, he was a corporate guy in a cubicle dreaming of becoming a teacher. So, at age 54 Dave took early retirement from Bell South and followed his dream. He finished his PhD in marketing and began teaching business classes at Nova Southeastern University and St. Leo College. Then he decided to take another jaunt into the corporate world with GTE. All the while, wine had nothing to do with Dave's professional life, but it had a lot to do with his personal life.

"I grew up with wine, I understood it," says Dave. "Everybody who is of Italian descent had a grandfather who made wine in the cellar." Dave was no exception.

He started out making wine from the fruit that grew in his backyard in Miami. In the late 1990s, he and his wife Ricky purchased land in Northeast Florida near the tiny town of Grandin. Dave wanted to do something with the land, but he wasn't sure what until a chance trip to Italy gave him the direction.

In 2003, after taking a river cruise in the south of France, Dave and Ricky got off the boat and decided to drive to the Italian Piedmont. With only his last name and the name of a village, they rented a car and headed into the countryside in search of his ancestral home.

After a crazy ride through the Italian mountains, they arrived in Calosso d'Asti where his grandfather had been born. Knowing almost no Italian, they somehow managed to tell their bed and breakfast hostess what they were searching for. She found six family members who had known his grandfather.

"It was amazing that we were able to meet them," says Dave, and even though communication was limited, he soon learned that they all grew grapes and made wine. "It put me over the top."

When Dave and Ricky returned to the states, they decided to turn the old Cracker house on the property into a winery. With its various rooms, the building was perfect for both a gift shop and wine production. Tangled Oaks Vineyard was born.

The works of local artists are featured at Tangled Oaks Vineyard.

"We built the winery on all things local," says Dave. "A local artist, Wendy Beeson, designed our wine labels and we like to feature local artists and locally made gifts in the shop."

In addition to the grapes they grow in their own vineyard, Tangled Oaks also buys grapes from local farmers and encourages and supports small vineyards.

"There is a definite difference between growing grapes and making wine and I'd rather not do both," Dave says. "I don't have the time. I'd rather be good at one thing."

That one thing is winemaking, and Dave is good at it. Just ask his customers. If that isn't enough, check out the medals his wines have won in competitions.

"A winery is really an integrated business," says Dave. "It's a combination of manufacturing, marketing, and selling. You take the raw materials, make your product, and then sell your product. You have to be prepared to do it all."

Dave says that growing the business was easy. The hard part was logistics. "I never thought I'd own a fork lift, trailers and trucks. Distribution is a challenge, and you have to make and sell enough wine to create a positive cash flow to pay for everything."

In addition to the on-site wine shop, Tangled Oaks Vineyard sells wine to small wine shops and local stores in North Florida from Jacksonville to Gainesville. Plans are to increase production and expand distribution beyond the local area. Currently annual wine production is about 2500 cases including both fruit wines and Muscadine grape wines.

Recently Dave's daughter-in-law Laura has come into the business, overseeing most of the winery operations from growing grapes to making wine to managing the winery and gift shop.

"I find myself wearing many hats," says Laura, who also has ideas for making Tangled Oaks a relaxing destination. "We want to create more sitting areas and garden areas, maybe even adding a pavilion. We want to be more of a 'happening' place."

Tangled Oaks Vineyard and Winery hosts two festivals each year, a spring festival in May and a fall festival in October. Both events include food, arts and crafts vendors, live music, and free wine tastings. Throughout the year, visitors can enjoy complimentary wine tasting, purchase wine to take home, or enjoy a glass of wine while relaxing in the garden overlooking the vineyard behind the winery.

Directions
From Palatka, take State Road 100 west about 18 miles to Tangled Oaks Vineyard and Winery on your left. From Interlachen, take County Road 315 north to Grandin about 13 miles, then turn right on State Road 100 and go about a quarter of a mile. The winery is on your right.

More garden and sitting areas make Tangled Oaks Vineyard a relaxing destination

Tangled Oaks Vineyard & Winery Wine List

Noble Red – made from the Muscadine Noble grape, this very fruity semi-sweet wine with a delicate balance is great with dinner or as an end of the day cocktail. Serve slightly chilled.

Carlos - a semi-sweet white Muscadine wine, made exclusively from the Carlos grapes with a refreshing bold flavor

Chardonnay – a dry white wine with a mellow, yet crisp, flavor that pairs well with any fish or chicken entree

Blueberry - a semi-sweet wine, made from fresh blueberries grown locally and still holding the true flavor of the fruit

River Oak Blueberry – this blueberry port wine is aged for 12 months with oak; very smooth with an exceptional flavor

River Oak Red – a smooth port aged twelve months in oak barrels

Bella Amie Blanc - made with Carlos grapes; a semi-dry full bodied white wine, matches well with fish and chicken

Spring Blush – breaking the mold of traditional blush wines with a zest of a Muscadine blend, semi-sweet and refreshing

Holiday Cheer - a sweet and refreshing blend of fresh berries that captures the spirit of any holiday

Florida's oldest dining car

While you're here...

Tangled Oaks Vineyard and Winery is located in the community of Grandin (population 200), about 18 miles west of Palatka on State Road 100. At the intersection of CR 315 and Highway 100 there is an old filling station and country store that was originally owned by long-time community resident Mr. Sykes who would wave to passers-by traveling the two roads. Once a gathering place for locals and folks who would stop by for a cold Coke, it has since been converted into a church. Today, the Palatka-Lake Butler State Trail runs along Highway 100 and right past the winery and the old store.

Area Information
Putnam County Chamber of Commerce
1100 Reid Street
Palatka, Florida 32177
386-328-1503
www.putnamcountychamber.com

Attractions
Palatka-Lake Butler State Trail
The trail is open daily 8:00 a.m. to sunset
There are no user fees
This rails-to-trails project uses the former Norfolk-Southern Railroad right-of-way through Putnam, Clay, Bradford and Union counties. Currently about 25 miles of the trail are paved, but eventually, it will be a 47-mile, multi-use recreational trail stretching from west of U.S. 17 in Palatka to State Road 238 in Lake Butler. It runs past Tangled Oaks Vineyard and Winery on the other side of Highway 100.

Etoniah Creek State Forest
390 Holloway Road (about 4 miles east of Tangled Oaks Winery)
Florahome, Florida 32140
386-329-2552
Over 8000 acres of natural areas off Highway 100 with three hiking trails that include a short half mile trail, a one-mile trail that leads to Lake George, and a 12-mile equestrian trail.

Palatka Railroad Preservation Society & David Browning Railroad Museum
222 N. 11th Street
Palatka, Florida 32177
386-328-0305 - www.railsofpalatka.org
Museum Open Monday – Friday, 9:00 a.m. to 5:00 p.m., Train layouts operate 1st Sunday and 3rd Saturday each month, 1:00 to 4:00 p.m. Historic photos and documents, railroad memorabilia, and HO scale model railroad with 16 operating trains

St. Johns River Center
102 N. First Street
Palatka, Florida 32177
386-328-2704
www.palatka-fl.gov/256/St-Johns-River-Center
Open Tuesday – Saturday, 11:00 a.m. to 4:00 p.m., Sunday 1:00 p.m. to 4:00 p.m.
Admission: Free, but donations happily accepted
Showcases the unique and varied ecosystems of the St. Johns River

Lodging
Crystal Cove Riverfront Resort
133 Crystal Cove Riverfront Resort Drive
Palatka, Florida 32177
386-325-1055
www.crystalcoveresortfl.com

Fun Eats
Angel's Dining Car
209 Reid Street
Palatka, Florida 32177
386-325-3927
Circa 1932 "Florida's oldest diner," curb service, burgers, and fries

"It was a happy gathering.
In my whole life,
I have never seen mead
enjoyed more
in any hall on earth."

- Beowulf

Royal Manor Meadery and Winery

Joe & Wanda Pasco
224 Royal Avenue
Interlachen, Florida 32148
386-916-8909 or 386-684-6270
www.royalmanorwinery.com

Hours: Tuesday – Saturday, 11:00 a.m. to 6:00 p.m.
Wine Tasting: $5, refundable toward a bottle purchase

My lords and ladies, hear ye. Be it known that fine meads and wines may be found in the humble village of Interlachen, and that ye may sample and purchase these delicacies for enjoyment in your own castle.

If ever you wanted to feel royal, a visit to Royal Manor Meadery and Winery will make you feel like a king or queen. Owned and operated by Joe and Wanda Pasco, Royal Manor is a bit of the Olde World in the heart of Old Florida.

Located on 30 acres at the end of a sandy road, Royal Manor presents a quiet country setting for sipping wine and watching the vines grow. For Joe, it presents the opportunity to experiment with fruit, explore flavors, and create liquid refreshments that bring his customers back for more.

Joe wasn't always a drinks-meister. In his various personas, he has been a chef, a fireman, a paramedic, and a constant seeker of knowledge and perfection. When his children were young, the family wanted to grow a backyard garden, but for Joe, who had never grown anything, it was more of a challenge.

"I'm not one to just make a garden," he says. "Joe's got to investigate. I asked myself, what have I got to do to make a really GOOD garden. Well, you got to get the pH right, so that's when I learned about pH and nutrient uptake. You can grow things with the pH off but it takes more nutrients and you're wasting your fertilizer."

The home garden was just the start, and soon Joe decided he could not only grow fruit, he could make wine out of it, so he set about learning how to make wine.

"Homeostasis is the perfect running of the human body," says Joe. "I learned that as a paramedic. When everything is running like clockwork, that's when you're in homeostasis. It's the same thing with yeast and making wine. Yeast has to have its own little homeostasis. When you make the perfect environment for that yeast to live, your wine will be perfect. And when you understand the whole concept of winemaking, then you can throw in your own creativity. Then you can say, 'how do I improve upon this?'"

He started with Muscadine grapes and blueberries and was soon winning awards as an amateur winemaker. One day a woman he knew who was making jams and sauces from kumquats challenged him to make a kumquat wine.

"All I knew about kumquats was that they were weapons to throw at your friends, but there's another softer, sweeter variety. So, once again there goes Joe – gonna learn everything he can about kumquats. I thought the sweeter ones would be better, but I was wrong. Those small, hard weapons make better wine."

In 2009, Royal Manor Vineyards had its first vintage, 240 gallons of Kumquat Royale wine. Other wines followed using such fruits as blueberries, blackberries, peaches, and even passion fruit. But no matter what he uses, Joe believes that maintaining the fruit flavor is most important.

"When you smell and taste my wines, they smell and taste like the fruit they are, and the only way to do that is to sweeten them," says Joe. "Sugar brings out the aromas and the flavors of fruit. That's why

God put sugar in the fruit. In order to make a really good fruit wine, you have to emulate the fruit."

In August 2010, Joe and Wanda opened the winery, offering more than a dozen different wines, and Joe continued to experiment with propagating various plants, including guava and fig trees a nd passion fruit vines. By then they had four acres of Muscadine and hybrid grapes planted and about 1000 blueberry bushes. Today, Royal Manor is a Certified Florida Farm Winery, with more than ten acres of fruit in production.

In 2012, they began making meads, which came as a natural extension of their Olde World theme and Joe's curiosity in fermenting honey. Some people think mead is beer, but mead is honey wine.

"Mead is the oldest alcoholic beverage in the world," Joe says. "Our forefathers – Thomas Jefferson, George Washington, Ben Franklin – they all made mead."

Joe makes traditional mead, which is basically honey and water, as well as fruit flavored meads such as blackberry, blueberry, and raspberry that are blended with the honey during fermentation. His meads have won gold and silver medals in international competitions, but more importantly, they have won him a loyal following of mead drinkers.

"I get compliments from people who drink mead all over the country," says Joe. "But, you can't please everybody, that's impossible.

I make my meads the way I want to drink them, kind of middle of the road sweet/dry. You can do that with a well-balanced wine."

Joes says mead is a niche market that is growing. To find that market, he takes his meads to Renaissance Fairs and Pirate Festivals all over the state.

"Pirates did not drink rum," says Joe. "That's a Hollywood thing. Rum was only available in the southern Caribbean. Period! Pirates drank mostly mead, they drank wine, and they drank all the port they could steal from the French and Spanish."

Joe says people are pleasantly surprised when they try mead for the first time and he usually sells out of whatever stock he takes to a festival. To increase production, he recently purchased an Italian-made bottling machine with a capacity to bottle 100 cases per hour.

With the meads and wines going well, Joe branched out again and set his sights on making hard cider; not just cider, but the best cider. Draggin Cider has 8% alcohol and is sold by the bottle (look for the dragon dragging an apple tree on the label) and by the keg, which has a shelf life of 90 days. He sells his cider at Royal Manor and also supplies a brewery in Gainesville.

By staying close to his original idea of fermenting fruit, Joe has managed to explore the related areas of wine, mead, and cider. He says he's bringing people into the market who might not have tried these drinks before.

"It's a passion and a challenge," he says. "It's about having fun and enjoying what you do, and about how you treat your customers. I treat all my customers the same, I care about them."

But, even with all his successes so far, Joe says he has no desire to corner the market. "I don't have to be the only one doing what I'm doing. I just want to be the best one."

Directions
From Palatka, take State Road 20 west about 12 miles to Twin Lakes Road. Turn left on Twin Lakes Road and follow the signs to Old Woods Road, Rodeo Drive, Clouds Avenue, Lake Road, and Carson Avenue to Addison Avenue. Turn right on Addison (this is a dirt road) and go to Royal Avenue. Turn right on Royal Avenue and follow it to the winery.

Royal Manor Meadery & Winery Wine List

All wines and meads are subject to availability

Wines
Kumquat Royale
Cherry Royale
Bayou Berry
Peach Panache
Royal Passion
Southern Passion
Berry Scintillating
Key Lime
Panacea Plum
Royal Blush
Mango
Sir Dud – blackberry wine
Sir Carlos – made from Carlos grapes
Nobility – dessert wine

Meads & Ciders

Traditional Mead	Spiced Mead	Draggin Cider
Zom-Bee Raspberry Mead	Cu Dubh Mead	
Blue Moon Blueberry Mead		

The Royal Manor

The suspension bridge at Ravine Gardens

While you're here...

The town of Interlachen is about 16 miles west of Palatka on State Road 20 in Putnam County. The name is Swiss meaning "Between the Lakes," and comes from the many clusters of inland lakes of various sizes scattered about the region. The town was developed by railroad executives as a winter resort area and was incorporated in 1888. Citrus farming and cattle ranching were the other two main industries. Today, Interlachen is a sleepy little former railroad town nestled in rolling hills between the lakes.

Area Information
Putnam County Chamber of Commerce
1100 Reid Street
Palatka, Florida 32177
386-328-1503
www.putnamcountychamber.com

Palatka Welcome Center
900 St. Johns Avenue (corner of St. Johns Avenue and Hwy 20, across from Dairy Queen)
Palatka, Florida 32177
386-328-0909
www.palatkadowntown.com
www.conleemurals.org - for a map and descriptions of the murals you'll see displayed around the downtown area.
Open Monday – Friday, 10:00 a.m. to 5:00 p.m.

Attractions

Ravine Gardens State Park
1600 Twigg Street
Palatka, Florida 32177
386-329-3721
Open daily 8:00 a.m. to sunset
Admission: $5 per vehicle
Features hiking trails, a suspension bridge, an interpretive center, a spring-fed creek, picnicking, a playground, and landscaped gardens

Interlachen Museum
311 Atlantic Avenue
Interlachen, Florida 32148
386-684-3811 Town Hall
Open Saturday, 10:00 a.m. to 2:00 p.m., group tours by request
Operated by Interlachen Historic Society, features history of the area

Carl Duval Moore State Forest
Trail Head Access is at 440 West Street, north of State Road 20
Interlachen, Florida 32148
386-329-2552
335 acres of sandhills, flatwoods, and a lake, 1.5-mile loop hiking and birding trail, and fishing dock – day use only

A mural on South 4th Street honors Billy Graham who started his ministry in Palatka.

Bronson-Mulholland House

100 Madison Street
Palatka, Florida 32177
386-326-2704
www.palatka-fl.gov/239/Bronson-Mulholland-House
Open Saturday, 10:00 a.m. to 4:00 p.m. and the 1st Sunday of each
month, 1:00 p.m. to 4:00 p.m., or by appointment
Admission: Free
Historic 1854 home of Judge Isaac Bronson, tours of the home and
gardens every half hour

Lodging
Crystal Cove Riverfront Resort

133 Crystal Cove Riverfront Resort Drive
Palatka, Florida 32177
386-325-1055
www.crystalcoveresortfl.com

Fun Eats
The Magnolia Cafe

705 St. Johns Avenue
Palatka, Florida 32177
386-530-2740
Breakfast, lunch, and coffee, paninis, sandwiches, and wraps

Shopping
Elsie Bell's Antique Mall

111 N. 4th Street
Palatka, Florida 32177
386-329-9669
www.elsiebellsantiquemalls.com
Featuring a variety of antiques and collectibles

Lady Bug's Gift Shoppe

114 S. 2nd Street
Palatka, Florida 32177
386-328-7502
Simply Southern merchandise, Mud Pie baby, and accessories, soy
candles, Melissa & Doug educational and classic toys

Bluefield Estate Winery

Bradley & Jennifer Ferguson
22 NE County Road 234
Gainesville, Florida 32641
352-337-2544
www.bluefieldestatewinery.com

Hours: Thursday & Friday, 11:00 a.m. to 5:00 p.m.
Saturday & Sunday, noon to 6:00 p.m.
Wine Tasting: $5 for four wines, $8 for eight wines

When your grandfather is legendary, it's a tough act to follow, especially if you are following along in the family business. For Bradley Ferguson, the family business is growing blueberries and his grandfather, Alto Straughn, is one of the most prominent farmers in Florida, and the largest blueberry grower in the state. With 16 total acres, Bradley and his wife Jennifer couldn't begin to compete, so they found an alternate path; they make blueberry wine.

"We started out using the fruit we couldn't sell in the fresh market," Jennifer explains. "We used imperfect berries and leftover fruit from Bradley's grandfather's farms and just started playing with it. It was hobby wine that we made in our kitchen, and our first batch was pretty mediocre, but we kept at it and kept improving it."

Today, their line of fruit fusion wines includes blueberries, strawberries, peaches, even pomegranate, and Muscadine grapes. The wines are made onsite in the couple's tasting room/winery surrounded by the vines and bushes that produce the berries, but originally, wine wasn't their business plan.

Both graduates of the University of Florida, the couple met and married, and moved to the farm as newlyweds. Immediately Bradley bought Jennifer a special gift. "My first love is horses," says Jennifer. "The first thing he bought me was a quarter horse."

They soon created a business of buying and selling horses and went on to collect nearly a dozen thoroughbreds and quarter horses. In addition, they began planting blueberries and grapes and Bluefield Estate was born. When it came time to create labels for the wines, horses were the obvious choice.

Bradley and Jennifer currently have an acre of blueberries and a little over an acre of Muscadine grapes, both Carlos and Noble varieties, under cultivation. The rest of the fruit for their wines comes from acreage Bradley manages on his grandfather's farms and from local growers. They also keep bees and produce honey, which they sell and use in the production of their wines. Bluefield Estate is a Certified Florida Farm Winery.

Blueberry bushes and Muscadine vines grow side by side at Bluefield Estate.

Bluefield Estate Winery offers a wide front porch for relaxing and sipping.

Even with so many different aspects to the business, Jennifer says the most grueling part was getting all the regulations in order. It took nearly 3 ½ years to satisfy all the state requirements to open the winery and to secure a distribution license to sell their wines to local businesses.

Today, Bradly and Jennifer make eleven different wines, producing about 5000 cases annually for sale in the winery and for distribution. They have plans to expand the operation, recently acquiring a piece of land on County Road 234, which will give them more visibility from the highway.

Bluefield Estate Winery is open four days a week for wine tasting. There is a tasting fee of $5 to taste four wines and $8 to taste eight wines. You can also purchase a bottle or two of your favorite wine and enjoy a glass on the large covered porch overlooking the vines and listening to the peace and quiet of the farm.

Directions
From Gainesville, take state road 20/S.E. Hawthorn Road to County Road 234. Turn left onto CR 234 and go about 3.7 miles to Bluefield Estate. Turn left onto the dirt road that leads to the winery.

Bluefield Estate Winery Wine List

Dry Blueberry – bold, fresh blueberry aroma, full-bodied, deep red color, chewy with a tart finish

Semi-Sweet Blueberry – fruity bouquet, medium body, smooth balance of sweetness and tart acidity

Sweet Blueberry – a fresh bouquet of berries, honey, and vanilla; medium body with a deep rich red color

Blackberry Bliss – a semi-sweet fruity fusion of Blackberry and Merlot

Green Apple Affair – like a green apple martini with initial tartness and a sweet, crisp finish

Peachy Perfection – distinct peach aroma and flavor that balances well with Chardonnay grapes resulting in a smooth fruity finish

Pomegranate Passion – the new superfruit balanced with Zinfandel grapes to give a hint of spicy sweetness

Raspberry Romance – sultry and sweet, a nicely balanced medium bodied wine with an amazing ruby color

Sweet Strawberry Sensation – a gentle blend of strawberry and white Zinfandel; a crisp and light blush wine

Windsor White – a semi sweet Muscadine wine made from the bronze skinned Carlos variety grapes; a light semi-sweet and aromatic wine.

Windsor Red – a traditional southern semi-sweet red, medium body, made from Noble Muscadine grapes

Mastodon skeleton at the Florida Museum

While you're here...

Bluefield Estate Winery, located in Alachua County, is right next door to the Gator Nation (that's the University of Florida for the uninitiated). Gainesville offers so much to do, from outdoor activities to cultural arts, history, and lots fun places to eat. Here are a few ideas to get you started in the area.

Area Information
Alachua County Visitors & Convention Bureau
30 E. University Avenue
Gainesville, Florida 32601
352-374-5260 or 1-866-778-5002 (toll free)
www.visitgainesville.com

Attractions
Florida Museum of Natural History
University of Florida Cultural Plaza
3215 Hull Road
Gainesville, Florida 32611
352-846-2000   - www.flmnh.ufl.edu
Open Monday – Saturday, 10:00 a.m. to 5:00 p.m., Sunday, 1:00 p.m. to 5:00 p.m.
Admission: Free for the museum – Admission to the Butterfly Rainforest is $13 for adults, $11 for Florida residents, college students, and seniors, and $6 for children ages 3 to17
See an ice age mastodon and other Florida fossils, wildlife, natural environments, waterways, and more in this family-friendly museum.

Harn Museum of Art
3259 Hull Road
Gainesville, Florida 32611
352-392-9826
www.harn.ufl.edu
Open Tuesday – Friday, 11:00 a.m. to 5:00 p.m., Saturday, 10:00 a.m.
to 5:00 p.m., Sunday, 1:00 to 5:00 p.m.
Admission: Free
This museum at the University of Florida features over 10,000 works
of African, Asian, modern and contemporary art, and photography.

Morningside Nature Center and Living History Farm
3540 E. University Avenue
Gainesville, Florida 32641
352-334-3326
www.visitgainesville.com/attractions/morningside-nature-center
Open daily 8:00 a.m. to 6:00 p.m. November through April and 8:00
a.m. to 8:00 p.m. May through October
Living History Farm open Monday – Saturday, 9:00 a.m. to 4:30 p.m.
More than six miles of trails wind through 278 acres of wildflowers
and long-leaf pine forests. The Living History Farm re-creates a single-
family rural holding in the year 1870 and includes a barn and one-
room schoolhouse, and an heirloom garden and live heritage breed
farm animals.

Newnans Lake Conservation Area
Trailheads on County Road 234 and County Road 26
1-800-451-7106 (toll free)
A 5,800-acre cypress-lined lake and wildlife preserve with ten miles
of trails for hiking, biking and horseback riding, picnicking and
primitive camping.

Gainesville-Hawthorne State Trail
3400 SE 15th Street
Gainesville, Florida 32641
352-466-3397
www.floridastateparks.org/trail/Gainesville-Hawthorne
Open dawn to dusk year round
This 16-mile long rails-to-trails project connects Gainesville to the
town of Hawthorne and is paved for bikes, pedestrians, wheelchairs,
and horseback riding.

Bed & Breakfast

Magnolia Plantation Bed & Breakfast Inn and Cottages
309 SE 7th Street
Gainesville, Florida 32601
352-375-6653 or 1-800-201-2379 (toll free)
www.magnoliabnb.com

Camellia Rose Inn
205 SE 7th Street
Gainesville, Florida 32601
352-395-7673
www.camelliaroseinn.com

Fun Eats

Flaco's Cuban Bakery
200 W. University Ave
Gainesville, Florida 32601
352-371-2000
Homemade Cuban sandwiches, hot entrees, beer and coffee

Adam's Rib Co.
2109 NW 13th Street
Gainesville, Florida 32609
352-373-8882
www.adamsribco.com
Breakfast, lunch, and dinner, ribs, BBQ, sandwiches, and burgers

Shopping

Waldo Farmer's and Flea Market
17805 U.S. Hwy 301
Waldo, Florida 32694
352-468-2255 - www.waldofleamarket.com
Featuring antiques, jewelry and everything under the sun

*"Wine is sure proof that God loves us
and wants us to be happy!"*

- *Benjamin Franklin*

Micanopy Winery & Countryside Vineyards

Matt & Crystal Bowman
22595 N. Highway 441
Micanopy, Florida 32667
352-234-0411 or 352-234-9519
www.floridavineyard.com

Hours: Call for appointment

Matt Bowman is comfortable at 30,000 feet. As both a Navy pilot and a business entrepreneur, he has no problem flying over challenges to get to the big picture. But, when it comes to getting the details in place, Matt has his feet firmly on the ground.

In this case, the ground is Matt and his wife Crystal's 20-acre farm located in northern Marion County mid-way between Ocala and Gainesville. Strategically placed and historically significant, the farm is a natural progression of life for a busy professional couple with deep roots in agriculture and a love of community and family.

"I'm a son of the South," says Matt. "My grandfather was a farmer and he owned land in the Gullah Geechee corridor of the South Carolina Low Country. Every summer, no matter where we were in the world, I was sent home to help work the farm."

Along with tending and harvesting the crops, Matt learned how to sell what he grew. His grandmother was the sales person and she'd take the orders and send Matt to deliver the produce. "You wouldn't think people would try to cheat a little kid, but sometimes I'd come up short of the cash. I had to learn to be tactful and say, 'no ma'am, that's not quite right.' I got really good at counting money," says Matt. "I learned how to get customers and how to keep customers, and most importantly, how to deliver what you say yo u're going to deliver."

In August and September Matt would help pick the Muscadine grapes that grew in abundance on his grandfather's farm. "My grandfather would make one batch of wine and we would open a bottle at Christmas. It was so good and so sweet, we thought of it as grape juice with a kick."

Matt graduated from high school and earned a scholarship to Florida A&M University to major in business. His father, a career Army man, insisted Matt enroll in ROTC. Even so, Matt had no intention of going into the military until the end of his third year when he got a call from a Navy recruiter. The Navy was recruiting pilots and they wanted Matt.

"My brother actually convinced me to do it," laughs Matt. "He said, 'look how young they all are, it can't be that hard.'" So, at age 20,

Matt signed up for the Navy.

Meanwhile, Matt had met Crystal, a Pharmacy major, and so began their life-long romance. "The Navy was the second best thing I found at FAMU," he says with a grin.

After graduation, Matt went to flight school in Pensacola, and later got his first assignment at NAS Whidby Island in Washington state. It was the mid-1990s and the wine industry in the Pacific Northwest was starting to emerge. Matt and Crystal met a local farmer and winemaker and were fascinated to see how quickly their business went from family farm to winery destination. "It gave us another appreciation for vine to wine," says Crystal.

From there, Matt and Crystal traveled all over the world to places like Hong Kong, Singapore, and the Middle East. Once they took a cruise to Greece, Italy, and Slovenia. "Everywhere we went, I was fascinated by how business is conducted. I also got to see how wine and local spirits are a part of the hospitality of each country."

The couple moved to Miami where Matt began running counter drug operations to Central America, which Crystal admits she wasn't thrilled about, but it helped them decide that after retirement from the Navy, they wanted to stay in Florida.

Crystal's family had owned land south of Gainesville since after the Civil War, so they decided to purchase several acres near some of the family holdings. When a property became available, they put in a bid and won out over a developer who wanted to subdivide it. Later, the property two doors down that had once belonged to Crystal's aunt became available and they immediately bought it.

"For us, it's more than creating an agribusiness," says Matt. "It's about continuing a tradition on family land."

When Matt's father, who now owns and operates Bowman Vineyards in Round O, South Carolina, asked him what he was going to do with his land, Matt's first thought was horses. "Marion County is horse country, so it seemed logical, but then growing fruits and vegetables won out. Micanopy was once the "bread basket" of the southeast with citrus and other fruits and vegetables," Matt explains.

Having helped his father with his vineyard, Matt decided to plant Muscadine grapes. They planted several rows of Carlos and Noble, with some Summit and Triumph varieties as well and started the Certified Florida Farm Winery process in 2013. He began making wines, experimenting with the brix and high quality water.

His winery concept began to emerge as well. Now, with three young children, Matt and Crystal have seen their lives change and become more family focused, so they decided they wanted to have an atmosphere for the whole family.

"We want to create a 'Florida Experience' for families to come and enjoy the country and learn about the history of the area. Micanopy was the first American city in Florida. That is, it was the first town incorporated after Florida became a state. Before that, it was Seminole land and we often find arrowheads out here."

Matt says there is also the remains of local blacksmith Toby Smith's shop on the property where they have found iron tools and bits of metal. The building that houses the winery was built in the 1950s of Ocala block, a type of concrete that used locally quarried limestone in the mix that creates a natural beige to salmon color.

At Micanopy Winery & Countryside Vineyards, visitors get a two-hour "Florida Experience" of history, agriculture, and wine, with a family focus. "We're bringing city dwellers to the country to relax, maybe take a hayride or a country cooking class, learn about winemaking, and walk through the fields and pick and eat fruits and vegetables fresh from the earth. With an emphasis on healthy eating, Matt says he is strictly organic and uses no pesticides or fertilizers in the naturally fertile soil.

The winery focuses on sweet to fruity wines, and Matt is currently making a Noble, a Carlos, and a blush. Using the native grape and locally sourced fruits, Matt is bringing his 30,000-foot idea down to earth. "We're making wines that completely reflect Florida," he says.

Directions
From Gainesville, take U.S. Highway 441 south for 15 miles. The winery is on the left.

Ancient, moss covered oaks create a cool, shady spot at Micanopy Winery.

Micanopy Winery & Countryside Vineyards Wine List

Noble – a light and fruity red wine made from the Noble Muscadine grape

Carlos – a sweet summer white wine made from the Carlos Muscadine grape

Blush – a fresh and fruity blend of the Noble and Carlos grapes

Historic Downtown Micanopy

While you're here...

Micanopy Winery and Countryside Vineyards is located 15 miles south of Gainesville on the Alachua County/Marion County line. The area is rich in natural resources and historical significance. The town of Micanopy is a wonderful place to spend the day antiquing and gallery hopping. For things to do in Marion County, see page 93.

Area Information
Alachua County Visitors & Convention Bureau
30 E. University Avenue
Gainesville, Florida 32601
352-374-5260 or 1-866-778-5002 (toll free)
www.visitgainesville.com

Attractions
Historic Downtown Micanopy
Located about ten miles south of Gainesville off U.S. Highway 441, Micanopy was founded in 1821 and named for a Seminole chief. It was the first town established in the new American territory of Florida. Here you'll find antiques shops, art galleries, and fun places to eat.

Micanopy Historical Society Museum
607 NE Cholokka Boulevard
Micanopy, Florida 32667
352-466-3200   - www.micanopyhistoricalsociety.com
Open daily 1:00 p.m. to 4:00 p.m. – Admission: $2 suggested donation
Artifacts of the history and everyday life in this pioneer town

Paynes Prairie Preserve State Park

Boardwalk overlook is on U.S. Highway 441
100 Savannah Boulevard
Micanopy, Florida 32667
352-466-3397
www.floridastateparks.org/park/Paynes-Prairie
Open daily year-round from 8:00 a.m. until sunset
Main Entrance Admission: $6.00 per vehicle
Named Florida's first state preserve in 1971, and now designated as a
National Natural Landmark, the park offers hiking, horseback riding,
wildlife viewing, camping, and picnicking.

Evinston Post Office and Country Store

18320 SE County Road 225
Evinston, Florida 32633
352-591-4100
Established in 1884, this is the oldest, continuously operating United
States Post Office in Florida. Housed in the Wood & Swink country
store, you can mail a letter, buy fresh produce or a jar of honey, and if
you're lucky, chat with local author and historian Fred Wood, Jr. and
buy a signed copy of his book, *Evinston... Home.*

Local author and historian Fred W. Wood, Jr. at the Wood and Swink store and Post Office

Kanapaha Botanical Gardens
4700 SW 58th Drive
Gainesville, Florida 32608
352-372-4981
www.kanapaha.org
Open daily except Thursday, 9:00 a.m. to 5:00 p.m.
Admission: $8 Adults, $4 Children ages 5 to 13, Children under 5 free
This botanical garden features 24 major collections visually accessible
from a 1 ½ mile paved walkway that include the state's largest public
display of bamboos and the largest herb garden in the Southeast.

Bed & Breakfast
Herlong Mansion Historic Inn & Gardens
402 NE Cholokka Boulevard
Micanopy, Florida 32667
352-466-3322
www.herlonginn.com

Fun Eats
The Depot/Antonio's
22050 N. U.S. 441
Micanopy, Florida 32667
352-591-0145
www.antonios.co/the-depot
Lunch and dinner - housed in a historic 1881 train station, featuring
authentic Italian food made with fresh, local ingredients

Mosswood Farm Store & Bakehouse
703 NE Cholokka Boulevard
Micanopy, Florida 32667
352-466-5002
www.mosswoodfarmstore.com
Freshly baked breads, pastries, coffees, and earth-friendly items

Shopping
Winters Past
116 NE Cholokka Boulevard
Micanopy, Florida 32667
352-545-7009
www.winterspast.com
Vintage clothing and jewelry

Island Grove Wine Company

Ken Patterson, Managing Member
Chase Marden, Winemaker
Robyn Aschliman, Operations Manager
Sarah Aschliman, General Manger
24703 SE 193rd Avenue
Hawthorne, Florida 32640
Office: 352-481-WINE (9463)
Tasting House: 352-481-1012
www.islandgrovewinecompany.com

Winery Hours: Monday – Friday, 10:00 a.m. to 4:00 p.m.
Winery Tours Monday – Friday, 11:00 a.m. and 2:00 p.m.

Tasting House Hours: Monday – Friday, 10:00 a.m. to 5:00 p.m.
Saturday 10:00 a.m. to 6:00 p.m.
Sunday 11:00 a.m. to 4:00 p.m.
Wine Tasting: Free

Long before U.S. Highway 301 connected the northeast United States to Central Florida's white-sand beaches, Island Grove really was an island. Surrounded by lakes, creeks and cypress swamps, the town was established in 1882 and grew from the thriving local citrus industry. By the late 1880s, thousands of pounds of oranges and vegetables were being shipped north each year by way of the Florida

Winemaker Chase Marden explains how the stainless steel tanks are used.

Railway and Navigation Company, the only means of transportation on or off the island other than by boat.

During the mid-20th Century, several years of hard winter freezes, citrus canker, and other events eventually put an end to what was once the largest citrus growing region in Florida, and local farmers looked to other crops.

Enter the mighty blueberry! Like the native Muscadine grapes, blueberries are hardy, healthy, and versatile. You can grow a lot more blueberries on the same tract of land that it takes to grow a fraction of the amount of other fruits. What's more, blueberries have been found to be high in – you guessed it – antioxidants.

So, in 1994, Ken Patterson and another local farmer decided to merge their two blueberry farms, and Island Grove Ag Products was born. One goal, along with producing top grade blueberries for the fresh market, was to establish a sustainable plant nursery to provide Florida native plants for growers.

They gradually acquired more of the surrounding land and began growing blueberries organically as well as experimenting with some University of Florida hybrids and low-chill varieties. They were growing plants, growing fruit, packing it, and shipping it all in one location.

In 2005, they established another farm about 175 miles south near Arcadia, Florida, the farthest south that blueberries will grow, and they began looking for ways to use the excess fruit left at the end of each growing season.

Enter Chase Marden, winemaker. Originally from the "frozen north "of Burlington, Vermont, Chase moved to Florida in the early 2000s looking to "fall in love with something," as he puts it. Always a science guy, he was fascinated by both the science and art of making wine.

"I got obsessed with it," he says. He began making various wines and opened his own winery in Largo, which he operated until 2005. Then, after working for another winery making various fruit wines, he arrived at Island Grove with the intention of making the best blueberry wine that he could make.

"Back in those days, it was all hand-done," says Chase. "We made the wine and fermented it in small batches. We hand bottled, hand labeled, it was very labor intensive."

In 2012, Island Grove Wine Company took a huge leap of faith. Investing in five 5000-gallon stainless steel tanks, and the automation needed to increase production, Island Grove expanded their wine production capability overnight to over 25,000 bottles. Today, total output is around 100,000 bottles per year.

Island Grove Wine Company makes two varieties of blueberry wines, and the names say it all; Kinda Dry and Sorta Sweet, which covers just about every taste. In addition to the high antioxidant content, the wines are low in sulfites and contain 100% blueberries, no fillers or flavorings.

Chase's experimenting has led to several fruit blended wines for which the winery purchases grape and fruit juices, but all production is done onsite. The Green Apple blended with Gewurztraminer is very popular as is the Raspberry blended with Zinfandel.

Today, Island Grove Ag Products maintains over 400 acres of blueberries, including 100 acres of organic blueberries, making the company the largest blueberry grower in the state. All packing and shipping of fresh fruit is still done onsite in their 17,000 square-foot packing house. Visitors can tour the winery production facilities on Fridays and taste wine overlooking the fields where the fruit is grown.

In addition to the winery, Island Grove Wine Company operates a Tasting House and gift shop on U.S. Highway 301 at the corner of County Road 325. There's a cozy tasting lounge with a bar, a fireplace, and a cushy sofa and chairs, All of Island Grove Wine Company's wines are available for tasting and purchase at the Tasting

House, and you can talk with the wine expert behind the bar about the wines.

The shop also carries wine gifts, tee-shirts, kitchen items, lots of fun cocktail napkins, and locally made products such as jams and jellies, salsas, and locally brewed beer. You can even taste locally made salad dressings and olive oils.

The little town of Island Grove, once a major player in the citrus industry, is still on the map. There are a few orange trees still producing their iconic Florida fruit, but the town itself is all but gone with the railroad. The next chapter belongs to the mighty blueberry.

Directions
Island Grove Wine Company Tasting Room is located at the corner of U.S. Highway 301 and South County Road 325 in the community of Island Grove.

To get to the farm winery and wine production facilities from the Tasting House, take U.S. Highway 301 north to SE 177th Avenue and turn right. Turn left onto SE 225th Drive, then turn right onto SE 177th Avenue. Turn right onto SE 243rd Street and go to the Island Grove gate. Turn left through the Gate and follow the road to the winery on your right.

A third location, Formosa Gardens, opened fall of 2017 at 3011 Formosa Gardens Boulevard in Kissimmee. Phone 407-507-9888

Blueberry bushes at Island Grove Wine Company

Island Grove Wine Company Wine List

Kinda Dry Blueberry – a medium-bodied, fruit-forward blueberry wine with a dark purple hue; pairs well with grilled steaks and chops

Sorta Sweet Blueberry – a light-bodied, fruit-forward wine with enticing aromas and flavors of fresh blueberry pie; goes well with barbecued chicken and grilled fish, or paired with desserts

Backporch Peach Chardonnay – light in body with a crisp, fresh finish, this fruit-forward wine pairs well with chicken and seafood and can be enjoyed before, with, or after dinner

Crisp Green Apple – sweet and crisp, a blend of Gewürztraminer and the light, fruity flavors of harvest-fresh green apples

Bold Blackberry – semi-sweet wine combines the medium-bodied dryness of a fine Merlot with ripe, sweet blackberries

Rustic Raspberry – vine-ripened raspberries and rich Zinfandel grapes provide this wine with its delightful fruity aroma

Southern Strawberry – a combination of tangy Riesling and fresh strawberries with a blush color, fruity aromas, and hint of sweetness

Blueberry Moscato – Muscat grapes and ripe, fresh blueberries together in a sweet, refreshing blend; serve with fruit-based desserts and mild-cheeses

Sunshine State Berry Sangria – a blend of oranges, lemons, limes, strawberries, blackberries and blueberries, aged with delicious Florida blueberry wine

Sunshine State White Sangria – a relaxing tropical blend of pineapple wine with mangoes and peaches

The Marjorie Kinnan Rawlings house

While you're here...

Island Grove Wine Company is located in south Alachua County on the shores of Orange Lake. Once a major citrus capital and a tourism crossroads, the area is rich in natural, "Old Florida" beauty and history, and was once the home of writer Marjorie Kinnan Rawlings.

Area Information
Alachua County Visitors & Convention Bureau
30 E. University Avenue
Gainesville, Florida 32601
352-374-5260 or 1-866-778-5002 (toll free)
www.visitgainesville.com

Attractions
Marjorie Kinnan Rawlings Historic State Park
18700 S. County Road 325
Cross Creek, Florida 32640
352-466-3672
www.floridastateparks.org/park/Marjorie-Kinnan-Rawlings
Park grounds open daily year-round from 9:00 a.m. to 5:00 p.m.
Guided tours of the house, Thursday through Sunday, from October through July on the hour starting at 10:00 a.m. until 4:00 p.m.
Park admission $3 per vehicle, house tours are $3.00 per adult; $2.00 for children, ages 6 to12; children aged 5 and under are free
Home of author Marjorie Kinnan Rawlings who wrote "The Yearling," this historic Cracker farm house has her original furnishings and is preserved and interpreted by the staff dressed in 1930s clothing.

Little Orange Creek Nature Park
24115 SE Hawthorne Road (Hwy 20, about 1.3 miles east of town)
Hawthorne, Florida 32640
352-481-2432 City of Hawthorne
www.littleorangecreek.org
Open daily, dawn until dusk – Admission free
This 1300-acre conservation-education-culture park features hiking
and horseback riding trails, birding, and a Nature Center that can be
rented for private and public events.

Bed & Breakfast
Laurel Oak Inn
221 SE 7th Street
Gainesville, Florida 32601
352-373-4535
www.laureloakinn.com

The Belvedere Farm Bed & Breakfast
13000 NW 90th Avenue
Reddick, Florida 32686
352-878-4069 or 352-816-2799
www.thebelviderefarm.com

Fun Eats
The Yearling Restaurant
14531 E. County Road 325
Hawthorne, Florida 32640
352-466-3999
www.yearlingrestaurant.net
Chicken, fish, deep fried clams, prime rib, venison, quail, frog legs, and
alligator

Shopping
The Orange Shop
18545 U.S. Highway 301
Citra, Florida 32113
1-800-672-6439
www.floridaorangeshop.com
Iconic shop selling fresh
Florida citrus and gifts since
1936

Antique Emporium of Florida
17990 NW 77th Avenue
Reddick, Florida 32686
352-591-1221
www.i75antiques.com
17,000 square feet of antiques and collectibles located off I-75 at exit 368

Island Grove Wines Tasting House Gift Shop
21848 S. County Road 325 (corner of U.S. Highway 301)
Island Grove, Florida 32640
352-481-1012
www.islandgrovetastinghouse.com
Wines and household gifts and décor

Spend a relaxing time shopping and tasting at Island Grove Wines Tasting House.

Katya Vineyards

David Sokol, Patricia Sokol, Katherine Sokol
101 E. Silver Springs Boulevard, Suite 102
Ocala, Florida 34470
352-528-2675
www.katyavineyards.com

Hours: Wednesday & Thursday, noon to 10:00 p.m.
Friday & Saturday, noon to 11:00 p.m.
Wine Tasting: $5 for four wines, $10 for eleven wines

A statistician, a college professor, and a ballerina walked into a winery and invited everyone to join them, because it was theirs. Of course, opening a family winery is no joke. The tale is far more complicated, but for the Sokol family, setting everyone's minds and diverse talents to the task was only the first step to success.

It all started in 2010 during a visit to her parents' small farm near Ocala. Katherine, a ballerina, was living the city life in New York. Her parents had retired from their careers in academia and the private sector and were deciding about the next phase of their lives.

"They sat me down and asked, 'how would you feel about starting a vineyard,' and I said if it means free wine for life, I'm totally game!"

For years, viniculture had been her father, David's, passion and armed with a PhD in statistics, he loved researching grape varieties and how they react to different winemaking methods. Katherine's mother, Patricia, also holds a doctorate degree and is the family business mastermind with a talent for organization and keeping everyone on track. As for Katherine herself, a Millennial with an arts degree, she is well versed in social media and marketing. The whole family has always had an enjoyment of fine wines, so as Katherine says, they all decided, "wine not!"

They purchased seven acres across the road from their farm and started a test vineyard of native Muscadines, even though they weren't sure they wanted to use those grapes for their wines. Still new to grape-growing, the vineyard didn't do well and they soon abandoned the idea.

Meanwhile, David's research led him to two hybrid varieties, Blanc du Bois and Lenoir, also known as Black Spanish. Soon they had added another 18 acres and hired a viticulturalist from Texas where Lenoir is widely grown to help them plant the vines. Four years later the vineyard was producing enough grapes for them to start the licensing and certification process for a commercial winery.

Katya Vineyards Tasting Room features a bar made from reclaimed wood.

David, known as Dr. Wine, approaches his winemaking both artistically and mathematically, and uses what is called fractional fermentation. Essentially, he varies the fermentation times and methods for each batch of juices, then blends them to create the wine flavors he wants.

There's a lot going on, from the grape/land connection, what the French call "terroir" or place where the grape is grown, to the subtle blending of juices to create the "profile" or flavor of the wine.

"We were looking for a Napa-style flavor profile, but from Florida," says Katherine. "We wanted to develop a profile that is specific to Ocala."

With the grapes growing and the wine fermenting, there was just one thing left to do, and that was to open the winery. Their first thought was to have a tasting room at the farm, but licensing and regulations were cumbersome and they soon realized that having a location in downtown Ocala would open more possibilities.

"We knew we wanted to have a tasting room, but we're learning as we go as far as being a brick and mortar," says Katherine. "We know how to make wine, but having retail space and creating a place to be is very different."

They decided to go with a Soho-loft idea, harkening back to Katherine's days in New York. Local craftsman Dana Foster was doing some remodeling of their farmhouse, so they asked him if he could build a bar and he agreed. Using reclaimed cherry wood from a factory in Georgia, and moldings and baseboards from a circa 1853 local building, the finished bar nearly spans the length of the 1200-square foot former office space located across the street from the Ocala town square. The building itself dates to 1923 and they have kept a lot of the original brickwork with the idea of "old meets new."

The large tasting room at the front includes the bar, tables, and cushy chairs for visitors to relax. Free WiFi and televisions lend a sort of "if Starbucks® sold wine" effect. The backroom houses fermenting tanks and barrels, and a bottling machine so visitors can experience the winemaking process first hand.

"We wanted to create a destination for locals to meet and gather – a hang-out," says Katherine. "The community is very supportive and we promote each other. We like to feature local products and unique things you can't find anywhere else, like our handcrafted wines."

Visitors to the Katya Vineyards Tasting Room are sure to notice the great bird of prey, a falcon, looking down on the room from atop the bar. This is the sokol, the bird, that is the family symbol.

"Our family roots are eastern European," Katherine explains. "In the Slavic languages, if you were a falconer, your last name was Sokol, much like a blacksmith being named Smith, so our symbol is a falcon. When we were first creating ideas for the winery, Dad wanted me to draw a falcon for the logo. I said I'm a dancer not an artist, but I doodled it on the back of a coffee-stained napkin in a Starbucks® in New York and he said it was perfect, don't change anything."

Katherine says they decided to name the wines for family members and family interests. "For instance, our reds are named for my nephew Nikolai and for Mikhail Baryshnikov, because he's my favorite dancer."

However, her parents caught her off guard with naming the white wines. They suggested Alexandra and Katya, and the decision was made before she realized that she'd agreed to her middle name and to a nickname for Katherine. With their focus on producing clean and pristine wines, they also decided to name the winery Katya, since Katherine is the Slavic word for pure. Pure≻ Katherine≻ Katya.

Laughing, Katherine readily admits she really does "own" the business, lock, stock, and label.

As for working with her parents, Katherine says it's an easy and natural thing to do, even though they are all perfectionists. Since they have each carved out a niche for themselves in the day to day operations of the business, they don't step on each other's toes when it comes to getting things done.

"My parents are very happy; they love it, I love it, and they gave me a job too," laughs Katherine. "We're building a family legacy."

Directions
Katya Vineyards Tasting Room is located at the corner of NE 1st Avenue and E. Silver Springs Boulevard in downtown Ocala.

Katya Vineyards Wine List

Red
Nikolai – American red blend that resembles a Zinfandel

Mikhail – American red blend that resembles a Cabernet

White
Katya – Their signature wine, an American white blend that resembles a Sauvignon blanc

Alexandra – American white blend that resembles a Chardonnay

Katya Vineyards Tasting Room is located in downtown Ocala.

*"Once, on a trek through Afghanistan,
we lost our corkscrew...and were compelled
to live on food and water for several days."*

- W. C. Fields (1880-1946)
American comedian, actor, juggler and writer
From the film "My Little Chickadee," 1940

The Corkscrew Winery

Joe & Kelli Carvalho
16 SW Broadway Street
Ocala, Florida 34471
352-402-0158
www.thecorkscrewwinery.com

Hours: Tuesday – Thursday, noon to 9:00 p.m.
Friday & Saturday, noon to 11:00 p.m.
Closed Sunday & Monday
Wine Tasting: $5 for three 2-ounce glasses

Of all the wine tools and accessories, the corkscrew is the most iconic. It has one purpose, to remove a cork from a bottle, so when Joe and Kellie Carvalho were planning to open their winery, The Corkscrew was the perfect name and image.

Located in downtown Ocala, The Corkscrew is a combination wine bar, winery, DIY drinks workshop, private venue rental, and live music stage that grew out of the couple's love of crafting good wine and good beer. They learned their craft in an unlikely place.

"We met while we were volunteering at a mission school in Belize," says Joe. "I'm from Canada and Kelli is from Ocala. There was another volunteer there who was a winemaker and the challenge was to find fruits that he could make wine from, since they don't grow grapes in Belize. We started experimenting with native, tropical fruits and spontaneous fermentation and got hooked on winemaking."

After getting married and settling in Ocala, Joe and Kelli decided to turn their love of winemaking into a business. They opened The Corkscrew in 2012 and soon they added craft beer to the mix. To share their passion with other like-minded people, they started conducting classes on wine and beer making.

"It takes four to eight weeks to complete a batch of wine, depending on the varietal you choose," says Joe. "Fruitier wines take less fermentation time, so you can have a batch of peach Chardonnay ready to bottle in about four weeks."

Both private and group classes are offered and The Corkscrew supplies all ingredients, corks, bottles, labels, and expertise for one fee. Then they "babysit" your wine until it's time to bottle it and take it home. For an additional fee, you can have custom labels made for special occasions, gifts, or just to serve to friends. Each batch of wine makes about 28 to 30 bottles. Private winemaking sessions are by reservation only. Beer making is similar in process and yields about five gallons, or about 50 bottles of beer.

The Corkscrew offers wine and beer making classes.

In addition to making your own craft wine or beer, you can enjoy a glass of Kelli and Joe's own vintages and brews. Continuing their experimenting with various fruits and blends, they currently produce several different red and white wines from grapes and juices brought in from locations around the country. They purchase locally grown blueberries and honey, and are working on crafting meads. They also maintain two Muscadine

vineyards just outside the city and are experimenting to make a drier, more intense Muscadine wine.

As for their beers, they grow their own hops and herbs and have created a variety of beers ranging from lager to a whiskey stout.

The Corkscrew Winery is open for wine and beer tastings Tuesday through Saturday. Each flight includes three pours of a selection of wine or beer that equal to about one glass. Or, you can simply enjoy the wine bar and order a glass of wine or beer for $5. On Friday and Saturday evenings, you can relax and enjoy the music of local musicians along with your brew or vino.

The Corkscrew Winery has a second location at 1171 Main Street, Lady Lake, Florida (at The Villages) 32159. The phone number there is 352-751-1787.

What started as an adventure to help other people in Belize has turned into a full-time business of helping other people in Ocala for Joe and Kelli. Joes says they wouldn't have it any other way. "It was providential."

Directions
The Corkscrew Winery is located on SW Broadway Street in Ocala, one block south of W. Silver Springs Boulevard, between SE Magnolia and SW 1st Avenue.

The Corkscrew Winery Wine List

Fruity Wines
Peach Chardonnay – a combination of ripe, sweet fruit and the smooth butteriness of Chardonnay

Blackberry Malbec – a slightly bold, fruity wine with intense fruit flavors of Malbec and refreshing notes of blackberry

Raspberry Merlot - invigorating fruit flavors of plump sun-ripened berries combined with the natural blackberry character of Merlot

Blueberry Pomegranate White Merlot - a combination of aromatics and flavors of red berry fruits found in White Merlot with that of the tangy blueberry and tart pomegranate

Green Apple Riesling – a crisp, crunchy green apple flavor with a pleasant initial tartness, followed by a delicious juicy finish

Blends
Cuvee Blanc – a boldly fruity wine from a blend of Chardonnay, Muscat, and Riesling

Cuvee Rouge - Dark purple in color with a nose of blackberry jam melded with creamy vanilla aromas

Whites

California Chardonnay	Australian Riesling
Italian Pinot Grigio	South African Sauvignon Blanc

Reds

Australian Shiraz	French Cabernet
Chilean Merlot	New Zealand Pinot Noir
Spanish Rioja	

Premier Reds

Sonoma Valley Pinot Noir	Napa Valley, Stag's Leap Merlot
Lodi Old Vines Zinfandel	Argentine Malbec
Red Mountain Cabernet	Italian Amarone
Spanish Tempranillo	

A Glass Bottom Boat at Silver Springs

While you're here...

The city of Ocala is in Marion County, Florida's Thoroughbred Country where horse farms and horses abound. Ocala is also the home of the iconic Florida attraction of the mid-20th Century, Silver Springs and its glass bottom boats. There is a lot to do here, so take your time.

Area Information
Ocala/Marion County Visitors and Convention Bureau
112 N. Magnolia Avenue
Ocala, Florida 34475
352-438-2800 or 1-888-356-2252 (toll free)
www.ocalamarion.com
Visit the website for self-guided horse farm tours

Attractions
The Canyons Zip Line & Canopy Tours
8045 NW Gainesville Road (County Road 25A)
Ocala, Florida 34472
352-351-9477 (ZIPS)
www.zipthecanyons.com
Open daily 9:00 a.m. to 6:00 p.m., last tour leaves at 3:30 p.m.
Pricing: zip tours range from $30 to $96, horseback tours are $59
Call for updated prices and opening hours
Billed as Florida's highest, fastest, and longest zip line tour. The Canyons is a converted phosphate mine that features nine different zips, two rope bridges, a rappel, and hiking trails. There is also horseback riding. All tours are led by certified guides.

Silver Springs State Park

5656 E. Silver Springs Boulevard
Silver Springs, Florida 34488
352-236-7148
www.floridastateparks.org/park/Silver-Springs
Park is open daily 8:00 a.m. to sunset year-round
Silver River Museum and Environmental Center is open weekends and major holidays from 9:00 a.m. to 5:00 p.m.
Admission to the park is $8 per vehicle plus a $2 per person admission to the museum, children under 6 are free
Glass Bottom Boat Tours are $11.00 for adults, $10.00 for students and seniors, and children under age 6 ride free
The iconic glass bottom boat ride park is still around and given a new lease on life as a Florida state park. Enjoy acres of paved walking paths through the gardens, wildlife viewing, picnicking, camping, and canoe and cabin rentals.

Appleton Museum of Art

4333 E. Silver Springs Boulevard
Ocala, Florida 34470
352-291-4455
www.appletonmuseum.org
Open Tuesday – Saturday, 10:00 a.m. to 5:00 p.m., Sunday, noon to 5:00 p.m., closed Monday
Admission: $8 Adults, $6 Seniors, $4 Children 10 to 18, Children 9 and under free
Over 30,000 square feet of gallery space featuring a permanent collection of European, American, Asian, African, Contemporary and pre-Columbian art and artifacts. Also, a collection of works of Florida artists reflecting the history and cultural heritage of Central Florida.

Bed & Breakfast
Belvedere Farm Bed & Breakfast
13000 NW 90th Avenue
Reddick, Florida 32686
352-878-4069 or 352-816-2799
www.thebelvederefarm.com

Fun Eats
Tavern on the Square
11 E. Silver Springs Boulevard
Ocala, Florida 34471
352-390-8969
www.tavernonthesquareocala.com
Lunch, brunch, and dinner menus featuring seafood, beef, and lamb

Stella's The Modern Pantry
20 SW Broadway Street
Ocala, Florida 34471
352-622-3663
www.stellasmodernpantry.com
Locally sourced ingredients for salads, sandwiches, and lighter fare

Shopping
Artist-Alley
108 E. Fort King Street
Ocala, Florida 34471
352-351-ARTS (2787)
www.artist-alley.com
Showcasing over a dozen artists, this art gallery features painting, photography, glass, jewelry, sculpture in a variety of media

Digger's Antique Mall
1811 N. Pine Avenue
Ocala, Florida 34475
352-629-5250
www.diggersantiquemall.com
A 9000-square foot showroom featuring furniture, décor, lamps, art, pottery, glass, antiques and collectibles from the last three centuries.

"You'll have no scandal
while you dine,
But honest talk
and wholesome wine."

- Alfred, Lord Tennyson (1809-1892)
Poet Laureate of Great Britain and Ireland
from "To The Rev F.D. Maurice"

Dakotah Winery

Rob Rittgers & Max Rittgers
14365 NW Highway 19
Chiefland, Florida 32626
352-493-9309
www.dakotahwinery.com

Hours: Monday – Saturday, 10:00 a.m. to 5:00 p.m.
Wine Tasting: Free

It's an eclectic mix of wagon wheels, old farm equipment, tools, barrels, wine presses, and potbellied stoves that greets you as you arrive at the winery. Inside, the display changes to locally made jams, jellies and sauces, gift items, glassware, and wine. The collections of a lifetime? Not quite, but for over 30 years Dakotah Winery has called this spot along U.S. Highway 19 home, and you know how things pile up around the house after a while. Fortunately, there's plenty of room and the items all add to the uniqueness of this roadside destination.

"People often bring us things because they know we collect certain items," says Rob Rittgers, owner and winemaker at Dakotah Winery. "They may have something like an old wine press from when their family made wine. They don't have a use for it, but they know we'll put it on display."

Along with family heirlooms, there are some old movie props

from a 1920s south Florida movie set, conquistador helmets and swords that were part of Dakotah Winery's early years of honoring Florida's winemaking history. Then there is the koi pond, a refuge for fish and fowl alike, where a living version of the winery's logo, a wood duck, can be seen in all its colorful glory.

Dakotah Winery began in 1985 with Rob's father Max Rittgers. Originally from South Dakotah, and a former Methodist minister, Max wanted to plant something useful on a piece of land he had acquired. He began by planting 200 Muscadine grape vines and sold the resulting grapes for both winemaking and to the fresh market. Rob soon came into the business to help his father as the wine grapes began to take precedence. They gradually added more land and replaced the eating grapes with winemaking grapes. Today, Dakotah Winery focuses exclusively on wine production and maintains over 20 acres of Carlos and Noble Muscadine vines in nearby Fanning Springs.

For Rob and Max, making use of the land is important. "We encourage people to plant whatever they can, whenever they can, be it a grapevine or a palm tree. It's important to take advantage of what the land has to offer."

For Max and Rob, the land offered plenty and by 1992 they had outgrown the original 8 by 10-foot shed where they had first started making their wines. They knew they needed a building that could grow with the business, but they also wanted a design that would reflect the area's "Old Florida" history. They settled on an expanded

Wine presses, barrels and wagon wheels on display at Dakotah Winery.

version of a Cracker farmhouse to serve as the tasting room, gift shop, and wine production facility, which they built next to the existing pond. They introduced the koi to the pond and created the bird sanctuary for the wood ducks and Canada geese. Eventually they added an events deck overlooking it all. Rob calls it a winery-slash-construction site. "We're always pounding nails and building something," he says.

In 2011, they decided to dig a wine cellar, not an easy feat in Florida where the water table is often not far below ground. They dug 4 ½ feet and, despite the nearby pond, didn't hit water. Encouraged, they continued to dig, creating a naturally cool space that today serves as the wine production and fermentation cellar.

As for their wines, Rob says they decided to not create fancy names but to stick with the varietals themselves. They have a red and a white Muscadine (Noble and Carlos) and a blush that is a blending of the two. Their Chardonnay, Merlot, and Cabernet are made from high quality grapes and juices from California growers, and they purchase locally grown fruits for their blueberry dessert wine. Dakotah Winery produces about 7000 gallons of wine annually, mostly the Muscadine varietals, which is what their customers like.

"We're a customer led business," says Rob. "We used to make our own jams and jellies, but we found that our customers liked our Noble wine the best. So, we scaled back our personal production of jellies, which we now buy locally, and concentrate on processing all the grapes we can get our hands on."

Rob says that they started the wine business with the idea of making an affordable wine that was easy and pleasant to drink. Like the grape growing and building construction, the winemaking grew and they learned from their mistakes. They got advice from the viniculture department at Florida A&M University and from winemakers at other wineries.

"Making wine is like cooking a recipe," says Rob. "There's a lot of information that's not necessarily in the recipe. You have to read between the lines." That's where the other wineries were so helpful in giving tips and suggestions and Rob encourages his customers to visit other wineries as well.

Dakotah Winery offers free tastings of their nine wines and their no-alcohol Muscadine juice. Their Carlos, Noble and Blush are mid-range, sweet table wines and their cream sherry, port, and blueberry are sweet dessert wines. Chardonnay, Merlot, and Cabernet

Sauvignon are drier wines in keeping with those European-style grapes.

Visitors to the winery are free to explore the grounds and the artifacts, relax in the courtyard, and enjoy watching the ducks and feeding the koi. There are tables and chairs and you may bring a picnic if you like, but Dakotah Winery's licensing does not allow for drinking on the premises. You may, however, purchase wine to take home with you.

While you browse the gift shop, be sure to look for the cedar door sill above the entry to the wine cellar. It was carved by a local artist from cedar trees that were felled during the 1993 "Storm of the Century" when eleven tornados hit Florida as the storm moved north up the coast. There's also the Dakotah Winery grapevine tree covered in unique Christmas ornaments for sale year-round.

As for Max and Rob, if you don't see them in the shop check down in the cellar where they're likely to be bottling more of their delicious wine. "It's a fun thing," says Rob. "We enjoy what we do."

Directions
Dakotah Winery is located on U.S. Highway 98/19, midway between Fanning Springs and Chiefland, about 5 miles either way.

Dakotah Winery Wine List

Cabernet Sauvignon – a rich, deep red, dry wine that easily pairs with your favorite steak

Merlot – a medium full bodied dry red wine with a hint of cherries and softer tannins

Noble - a red, semi-sweet table wine made from very dark flat black colored Muscadine grapes

Chardonnay - aged in stainless steel tanks for three years resulting in a lighter body, crisp, dry, white wine

Carlos – a slightly sweet, Muscadine table wine

Blush - a blend of the grapey Carlos white and semi-sweet Noble red, resulting in a perfect summer picnic wine

Blueberry - a sweet blueberry desert wine with a slight tart finish

Cream Sherry – a sweet cream sherry with a very nutty, pecan like taste

Port – an excellent port made from late harvest Noble Muscadine grapes, slowly fermented, brandy added and barrel aged three years

Muscadine Juice – non-alcoholic pure Muscadine juice

The Suwannee River at Fanning Springs State Park

While you're here...

Dakotah Vineyards and Winery is located in Levy County not far from where the Suwannee River winds its way to the Gulf of Mexico. The area bills itself as the Nature Coast and is rich in natural resources. Rivers and streams, natural springs, and forests are prevalent. Historically, farming and logging were the main occupations. Today, Cedar Key on the gulf coast attracts tourists, boaters, and anglers while the state parks lure hikers, swimmers, divers, and picnickers for a day in the outdoors.

Area Information
Levy County Visitors Bureau
620 N. Hathaway Ave.
Bronson, Florida 32621
352-486-3396
www.visitnaturecoast.com

Attractions
Fanning Springs State Park
18020 NW Highway 19
Fanning Springs, Florida 32693
352-463-3420
www.floridastateparks.org/park/Fanning-Springs
Open daily 8:00 a.m. to sunset year round
Admission: $6 per vehicle, cabin rentals $100 a night
Swimming, snorkeling, hiking, picnicking, wildlife viewing, and scuba diving at this second magnitude spring on the Suwannee River.

Manatee Springs State Park
11650 NW 115th Street
Chiefland, Florida 32626
352-493-6072
www.floridastateparks.org/park/Manatee-Springs
Open daily 8:00 a.m. to sunset year round
Admission: $6 per vehicle, camping $20 per night
The park is located on the Suwannee River and includes a first magnitude spring for swimming, snorkeling, and scuba diving. There are hiking trails, picnic sites, canoe and kayak rentals, wildlife viewing, and ranger led tours.

Nature Coast State Trail
352-535-5181
www.dep.state.fl.us/gwt/state/nat/default.htm
Open daily 8:00 a.m. to sunset year round
Admission: Free
This rails-to-trails project provides nearly 32 miles of paved trail for walking, bicycling, and horseback riding. The trail crosses the Suwannee River on the original train trestle bridge not far from the Old Town trailhead. Other trailheads are in Chiefland, Fanning Springs, Trenton, and Cross City near the Putnam Lodge.

The original train trestle bridge crosses the Suwannee River near Old Town on the Nature Coast State Trail.

Levy County Quilt Museum
11050 NW 10th Avenue
Chiefland, Florida 32626
352-493-2801
www.levycountyquiltmuseum.org
Open Tuesday – Saturday, 10:00 a.m. to 3:00 p.m.
Admission: Free
Quilts and quilt blocks from local crafters past and present are on display at this fabric arts museum. Quilts and other handmade items are also available for purchase.

Bed & Breakfast
Putman Lodge Hotel & Spa
15487 NW Highway 19
Cross City, Florida 32628
352-440-0414
www.putnamlodge.com

Fun Eats
19/98 Grill & Country Store
17110 NW Highway 19
Fanning Springs, Florida 32693
352-463-1998
www.1998grill.com
Fresh baked pastries and home cooked Southern fare

Treasure Camp on the Suwannee
15249 NW 46th Lane
Chiefland, Florida 32626
352-493-7607
Twelve miles south of Chiefland in Flowers Bluff and located on the Suwannee River. Serves seafood and American fare

Shopping
Point of View
17452 NW Highway 19
Fanning Springs, Florida 32693
352-463-0718
www.pointofviewgifts.com
Showcasing antiques, collectibles and works of local artists

Mitillini Vineyards

Michael Bresk & Annemarie Croucher
17569 Mitchell Road
Live Oak, Florida 32060
386-364-1773

Hours: Call for appointment

The idea began in a Greek restaurant with a placemat beneath a glass of wine. Depicted was a map of the Greek islands, the place names beckoning them like Sirens on the rocks. They talked all through the Moussaka about growing things and having a place of their own, and by the time the Finikia arrived they had a plan.

"Our retirement plan," says Michael with a grin. "We were tired of the city – too many people, too busy - and we wanted to find our roots in the country."

So, forsaking the beach life of Fort Lauderdale, they started looking for land and teaching jobs in North Florida. They found both not far from the banks of the Suwanee River in Live Oak. To make such a drastic change in lifestyle might be daunting to many people, but for

Michael and Annemarie, it's just another challenge. As an Irish lass from County Cork, Annemarie came to America in search of a new life, bringing her teaching skills with her. The contrast of Florida's warm climate to Ireland's chilly, wet winters sealed the deal.

Michael spent 25 years in Ohio in the world of accounting before deciding to trade in his spreadsheets for attendance rolls. He got his teaching certification and moved to Florida, where he and Annemarie met.

Today, Annemarie teaches first grade at Suwanee Primary School, and Michael teaches math at Suwanee High School. For both of them, teaching fulfills a need, a way of making a personal impact in the lives of others.

As for why they chose to grow grapes and make wine, it was kind of a "why not" moment, and once again they faced the challenge head on.

"We, of course had grown gardens, but never anything on this scale," says Annemarie. "Also, we'd never made wine. It's the challenge, I think. I love a challenge."

The challenge meant learning everything they could about first growing grapes, and then making wine. For Michael, a teetotaler for health reasons, the challenge was to grow wine grapes that would make great wine. For Annemarie, it's taking those grapes and creating the finished product.

"I grow the grapes and she makes the wine," grins Michael. "Easy, right?"

In 2005, the couple purchased 20 acres just outside Live Oak and soon they were planting their first vineyard. They decided to stay with native Muscadine grapes, which turned out to be a good choice. The rich soil was perfect for cultivation and the vines grew rapidly. They planted more vines and Michael was kept busy pruning and training his young plants. Each year's harvest yielded more grapes and they sold to the fresh market, u-pick, and to other wineries.

They currently have 10 acres under cultivation with nearly 1,800 vines. Production is about 8,000 pounds of both Carlos and Noble Muscadine grapes annually. With the advent of the winery, they are now using most of what they grow and expect to produce about 4000 gallons of Mitillini Vineyards wine per year.

Michael and Annemarie have done everything from planting to pruning to picking to building design and construction for the wine shop. As the tasting room nears completion, Michael is also managing the procedures and paperwork to obtain the necessary permits and licensing. Meanwhile, Annemarie works on decorating the tasting room and in securing suppliers to help stock the shop.

"Along with our wines, we plan to showcase local crafters and artists and feature locally made products," she explains. She plans to sell Muscadine jams and goat cheese along with other locally made items in the shop.

The couple also believes in creating a destination for visitors to come and spend a day in the vineyard. A koi pond at the front of the property offers children and the young at heart an opportunity to feed the fish. Visitors can also bring a picnic lunch and enjoy the peaceful surroundings of the countryside.

They also plan to host events and have already had several weddings in the vineyard, which is popular with brides looking for an outdoor setting. Photographers love the "old world" atmosphere.

"We've hosted some small weddings for 30 or so people," says Michael. "The cost is very reasonable and brides can have their own caterers and set up tables and tents if they want. We've constructed a trellis with the vineyard as a backdrop which makes for beautiful photos, especially from May through September when the vines are full of grapes." They have also hosted outdoor concerts featuring local musicians.

The view between the vines is reminiscent of old world vineyards.

With their full-time teaching jobs, the winery as a reality has been slow in coming, but Michael and Annemarie have already felt the pride of ownership and of making something good for the community. It's been a challenge, but one they happily accept.

Directions
From U.S. Highway 90 just west of Live Oak, turn onto 76th Street (Mitchell Road) and head west for about 5 miles until you see the Mitillini Vineyards sign on your right.

Mitillini Vineyards Wine List

Mitillini Noble – a semi-sweet red wine made from the Noble grape

Mitillini Carlos – a semi-sweet white wine made with the Carlos grape

Way down upon the Suwannee River State Park

While you're here...

Mitillini Vineyards is located in Live Oak in Suwannee County just off Interstate 10. Bounded on the north and west by the historic Suwannee River, and offering a multitude of parks, conservation areas, and natural springs, the region is perfect for birding and wildlife viewing, canoeing, hiking, swimming, diving, and other outdoor recreation.

Area Information
Suwannee County Chamber of Commerce
212 N. Ohio Avenue
Live Oak, Florida 32064
386-362-3071
www.suwanneechamber.com

Attractions
Suwannee River State Park
3631 201st Path
Live Oak, Florida 32060
386-362-2746
www.floridastateparks.org/park/Suwannee-River
Open daily from 8:00 a.m. until sunset
Admission: $5 per vehicle day use
Hiking and bicycling trails, birding, picnicking, camping, cabin rentals, and boating on the Suwannee River

Stephen Foster Folk Culture Center and State Park
11016 Lillian Saunders Drive/ U.S. Highway 41 North
White Springs, Florida 32096
386-397-4331
www.floridastateparks.org/park/Stephen-Foster
Park open daily 8:00 a.m. to sunset
Museum and Tower open daily 9:00 a.m. to 5:00 p.m.
Admission: $5 per vehicle, camping and cabin rental additional
The park honors the memory of Stephen Foster who wrote the song that made the Suwannee River famous. A 97-bell carillon plays Foster's music and skilled artisans demonstrate stained glass making, blacksmithing, quilting, and other crafts in Craft Square.

Big Shoals State Park
18738 SE 94th Street
White Springs, Florida 32096
386-397-4331
www.floridastateparks.org/park/Big-Shoals
Open daily 8:00 a.m. to sunset
Admission: $4 per vehicle
Featuring 28 miles of hiking trails and the largest whitewater rapids in Florida.

Spirit of Suwannee Music Park
9379 County Road 132
Live Oak, Florida 32060
1-800-224-5656 (toll free)
www.musicliveshere.com
A resort, music venue, festival site, and activity destination rolled into one. Live music nightly, craft village, camping, cabin rentals, restaurant with dinner theater, and swimming and kayaking in the Suwannee River.

Suwannee Springs
3243 91st Drive
Live Oak, Florida 32060
386-362-1001
Open daily
Admission: Free
A 135-acre park on the banks of the Suwannee River featuring the ruins of a 19th Century bathhouse that contains a natural sulfur spring.

Fun Eats
Down Town Café
229 W. Howard Street
Live Oak, Florida 32064
386-330-0320
Breakfast, lunch, and coffee serving sandwiches, wraps, homemade soups, salads and desserts

All Decked Out
1040 Duval Street NE
Live Oak, Florida 32064
386-362-7752
Serving lunch and dinner, seafood and hush puppies

Shopping
B' Posh
101 N. Ohio Avenue
Live Oak, Florida 32064
386-219-0281
www.bposhboutique.com
Boutique featuring ladies wear and accessories

The Busy Bee
6458 U.S. Highway 129 (I-10 exit 283)
Live Oak, Florida 32060
386-487-2935 - www.shopthebusybee.com
A super-sized convenience store with a gourmet chocolate bar

Even the bathrooms are fancy at the Busy Bee

"Good wine is a necessity of life."

\- *Thomas Jefferson*

Monticello Vineyards & Winery

Cynthia Connolly
1211 Waukeenah Highway
Monticello, Florida 32344
850-294-WINE (9463)
www.monticellowinery.com

Hours: Saturday – Monday, 8:00 a.m. to 6:00 p.m.
Call to make sure someone's there or to set an appointment
Wine Tasting: Free

What Cynthia Connolly really wanted to study was agriculture, so she went to Florida State University, in one of the best agricultural areas in the state, and got a degree in - English. In the early 1970s, agriculture wasn't an academic option for women, but as a horse lover and an outdoors person, Cynthia had a dream of one day owning a farm and growing things.

So, she had what she called a "Eureka moment!" She decided to go back for a second Bachelor's degree, this time in Technical Agriculture, but as a woman in a non-traditional field, there were few job options. She eventually ended up at Iowa State University's

College of Agriculture, one of the few graduate schools offering places to women, and earned her Ph.D. in Agricultural Education and Agricultural Engineering, concentrating in agricultural construction and mechanics. She was the first woman in the country to earn a Ph.D. in this field.

"I loved it! I knew I was in the right place," she declares. "I was interested in helping women internationally to have their own farms and grow better crops, and I knew this was the way to do it."

Cynthia did her doctoral research while teaching food production to women in the Sudan, which turned out to be the first of many overseas assignments over the next several years. She also worked for the U.S. Department of Agriculture, the United Nations Development Program, the United Nations Food and Agriculture Organization and the CIAT (Centro Internacional de Agricultura Tropical), the International Center for Tropical Agriculture where she spent several years in Colombia, South America developing training materials and working on a Biological Nitrogen Fixation project. Through all this, Cynthia always knew she wanted to come back to Tallahassee. When she was home on vacations, she would drive up and down country roads looking for a farm.

Then in August 1989, she found her dream just south of the town of Monticello in the Red Hills region of Jefferson County. She knew immediately that the 50-acre farm was perfect and she just couldn't leave. Cynthia laughs at the memory of that moment.

"I spent ten minutes looking at the farm and three hours getting the car out of the ditch," she says. But, having managed to back the car into a ditch wasn't a bad thing. "I knew it was meant to be. It was like the farm chose me."

At the time, Cynthia was still working in Colombia, but it was getting more dangerous to be there. In February 1990, she made the decision to move to the farm and grow food.

As an admirer of biologist, ecologist and writer Rachel Carson, Cynthia's goal was to be organic and do no harm to the earth. In those days, the idea of organic farming was not taken seriously, but to Cynthia, working with nature made more sense than trying to conquer it, so she created her company, Ladybird Organics. The name Ladybird comes from Ladybird beetles, also known as ladybugs, which are voracious predators of aphids and other pests; they are also a symbol of good luck the world over and show how a natural balance of prey and predator is the best pest control.

Cynthia decided to grow a variety of fruits and vegetables including grapes. She also teamed up with a local farmer, Al Leatherman, who was interested in grain production. Al helped her fix her barn and then they bought a combine. At the same time, Florida A & M University (FAMU) had started a program to help growers establish vineyards, so Al helped her plant a third of an acre of vines. She also planted a small orchard and a variety of vegetables.

Unfortunately, it wasn't long before Cynthia found she'd developed an allergy to grain dust, so she backed away from grain production. Vegetables proved to be a lot of work for little money, but the grapes grew, hardy and abundant. She planted more vines and sold the grapes as fresh fruit. She also made grape jam, but she felt the grapes had other plans.

"Grapes want to be wine," she says. "So, we made wine."

During her international work and travels, Cynthia spent a year in Rome. She says in Italy, wine is like food and a part of daily life. Muscadine grapes, which are native to the Southeastern United States,

have a distinct flavor, very different from the European grapes. However, unlike the European grapes, Muscadines thrive and grow well in our heat, humidity, and sandy soils.

"I wanted to make a wine that I liked to drink using Muscadine grapes," says Cynthia, so she set out to make a drier wine from the naturally sweet fruit.

As with all the fruits and vegetables grown on the farm, the grapes are grown organically with no pesticides, herbicides or chemical fertilizers. In fact, as in everything else she does, Cynthia took an academic approach and researched, studied and be came an expert in vermiculture, otherwise known as worm farming.

"Worm castings are an excellent organic fertilizer for the vines and one of the best nutritional sources for growing everything," Cynthia explains. She says the best fruits are produced in an organic production system, and that the best fruit makes the best wine.

Monticello Vineyards & Winery was Florida's first organic farm winery. It became a certified Florida Farm Winery in 2001. Cynthia keeps 10 acres planted with 18 different varieties of grapes. She uses three main varieties to make her wines, Carlos, Magnolia and Ison, and experiments with other varieties like Triumph and Welder on a limited basis. The wines range from semi-sweet to dry and have a distinct Muscadine bouquet.

"Muscadine grapes are very nutritious - full of bioflavonoids and antioxidants like the exotic fruits from the tropics," Cynthia explains. "The health benefits are in the wine as well. Fermentation actually helps concentrate some of the health prope rties like Resveratrol. Using certified organic grapes to make the wine assures that there are no residues from toxic sprays or chemicals used in production."

As a one-woman show, Cynthia keeps her wine production at about 1000 gallons annually. All of her wines are made using 100% fresh pressed juice, from USDA certified organic grapes that are hand-picked, crushed and fermented all onsite with the help of volunteers.

"I've burned out a lot of friends and family at harvest," Cynthia laughs, but she adds, "I am always amazed at how people are willing to roll up their sleeves and pitch in and help."

Wine sales are both online and out of a small wine shop nestled among the vines. Cynthia offers wine tastings Saturday, Sunday and Monday, but she advises visitors to call ahead and it's best to make an appointment.

Ladybird Organics is also a Certified Nursery and Cynthia sells Muscadine vines, and worms and worm castings for gardeners and people wanting to start their own vineyard or vermiculture project. In addition to everything else, Cynthia is also an Organic Inspector who has worked with other farms and farmers applying to become USDA certified organic. The lady who wanted to be a farmer now grows foods for her community and beyond, and welcomes the public to try her fresh organic grapes and the unique Muscadine wines made from them.

Directions
From Interstate 10, take Exit 225 and go north on U.S. Highway 19 for about 3 miles to Waukeenah Highway (county road 259). Turn left and go one mile. The entrance to the winery is on your left.

Monticello Vineyards little tasting barn sits among the vines.

Monticello Vineyards & Winery Wine List

Florida Red– A traditional bold Muscadine, this red wine is fruity and flavorful. Made from organically grown Ison grapes, *Florida Red* is available in both a dry and a semi-sweet wine.

Magnolia – Think "Old South" when you sip this well balanced, white wine that comes from one of the older, varieties of Muscadine grape, Magnolia. A floral finish and subtle sweetness make this wine a favorite of those seeking a slightly sweeter wine, but a dry version is also available.

Carlos - A crisp, clear, dry and fruity white wine made from the variety of Muscadine grape called Carlos, this wine is available in a dry or a semi-sweet wine.

White Muscadine Blend - several varieties of white Muscadine grapes are blended to make this delicate, fruity, and dry wine

The Monticello Opera House is said to be haunted.

While you're here...

Named for the third President of the United States, Jefferson County was established in 1827. The county seat is named for Jefferson's home, Monticello, but here it's pronounced "Monti-sello." With many buildings listed on the National Register of Historic Places, Monticello is the quintessential "old Southern" town. It also has the distinction of being named the "South's Most Haunted Small Town" by PBS-TV and "The Most Haunted Small Town in America" by ABC-TV News. Ghost tours are offered the last Saturday of each month and three weekends in October.

Area Information
Jefferson County Tourist Development Council
420 W. Washington Street
Monticello, Florida 32344
850-997-5552
www.visitjeffersoncountyflorida.org

Attractions
Monticello
Take a walking and driving tour of this historic town that dates back to a time before Florida was a state. See the 1833 Wirick-Simmons House, the 1875 Register's Barber Shop, the beautiful 1885 Christ Episcopal Church, and the 1890 Monticello/Perkins Opera House, one of several buildings in town believed to be haunted. The Chamber of Commerce has a free brochure that lists all the houses and buildings along with a tour map.

Letchworth-Love Mounds Archaeological State Park
4500 Sunray Road S. (off U.S. Highway 90, 6 miles west of Monticello)
Monticello, Florida 32309
850-922-6007
www.floridastateparks.org/park/Letchworth
Open daily 8:00 a.m. to sunset
Admission: $3 per vehicle
Florida's tallest Native American ceremonial mound, built between 1100 and 1800 years ago. Park includes a picnic pavilion with an interpretive display and a nature trail and boardwalk

Bed & Breakfast
Avera-Clarke House Bed & Breakfast
580 W. Washington Street (U.S. Highway 90),
Monticello, Florida 32345
850-997-5007
www.averaclarke.com

John Denham House
555 W. Palmer Mill Road
Monticello, Florida 32344
850-997-4568
www.johndenhamhouse.com

The John Denham House is one of several purportedly haunted B&Bs in town.

Fun Eats
Brick House Eatery
190 N. Jefferson Street
Monticello, Florida 32344
850-997-2100
Café serving homemade soups, salads, sandwiches, and desserts

Tupelo's Bakery & Café
220 W. Washington Street
Monticello, Florida 32344
850-997-2127
www.tupelosbakery.com
Tupelo's serves sandwiches, salads, desserts, and baked goods made with 100% organic ingredients.

Shopping
Huckleberry's Creations
210 W. Washington Street
Monticello, Florida 32344
850-528-1339 or 850-997-3400
Huckleberry's features painted furniture, antiques, and gifts.

Jackson's Drug Store
166 E. Dogwood Street
Monticello, Florida 32344
850-997-3553
Find cards, gifts, and sundries at this old fashioned drug store.

Vintage Treasures
235 N. Jefferson Street
Monticello, Florida 32344
850-997-1520
www.vintagetreasures235.com
Antiques and collectibles, furniture, jewelry, and handcrafted items housed in an historic building

FAMU Viticulture Center

Since the 19th Century, state universities have played a significant role in the development of the Florida grape and wine industry. Research during the 20th Century at the University of Florida in Gainesville produced some of the best known hybrid grapes planted throughout the country today. In 1978, with encouragement from the Florida Grape Growers Association, the Florida Legislature established the Center for Viticulture and Small Fruit Research at Florida A&M University in Tallahassee. With an emphasis on developement and improvement of native and hybrid grape varieties, the FAMU Viticulture Center has grown to be one of the top grape research facilities in the country.

The center is located just east of Tallahassee on Highway 90 off Interstate 10 at what was the former Lafayette Winery. The land, approximately 50 acres, was once owned by the Marquis de Lafayette who established vineyards in the early 1800s with the intention of growing grapes for winemaking. Today, the FAMU Viticulture Center is housed in a 15,000 square-foot state of the art laboratory and grows dozens of different kinds of grapes.

In addition to focusing on traditional breeding practices, biotechnology, and invitro selection of healthy grape varieties, FAMU faculty and students provide research, training, and support for grape and small fruit growers through a number of extension and outreach programs. These include vineyard establishment and management practices, on-site vineyard inspections, and workshops in pesticide safety, canopy management, and pruning among others. The center also assists in developing grape products (including wine) for the commercial market and in marketing grapes and wine.

The Southeastern Regional Center of the National Clean Plant Network (NCPN) for Grape is also located here which develops and grows high quality grapevines that are free of common grapevine diseases such as Pierson's Disease. The center supplies these vines to the viticulture industry across the southeast.

Once a year, the FAMU Viticulture Center opens its doors to the public for an old fashion day of fun in the vineyard. The Florida A&M University Grape Harvest Festival occurs around the end of August or early September to celebrate the grape. This family-friendly event features a grape stomping contest, a kids' petting zoo, a health fair, water slides, a grape throwing competition, and 5K run though the vineyard. There are also vineyard tours, wine sampling, and a home winemaking workshop.

The Center for Viticulture and Small Fruit Research can be contacted for advice on growing grapes and other small fruits. Their website offers free, downloadable instruction guides and Power Point presentations on pesticide safety, canopy management for grape vineyards, and fruit tree pruning and training. There's also a 62-page production and marketing guide for Muscadine grapes in Florida.

Center for Viticulture and Small Fruit Research
6361 Mahon Drive
Tallahassee, Florida 32317
850-599-3996
www.famu.edu/index.cfm?viticulture

A day in the vineyard at the FAMU Viticulture Center

*"I love everything that is old:
old friends, old times, old manners,
old books, old wines."*

*- Oliver Goldsmith (1730-1774)
Irish novelist, playwright and poet
from "She Stoops to Conquer"*

Old Oaks Vineyard

Bridget Keegan
1536 Will Lee Road
Bonifay, Florida 32425
850-547-2254
www.oldoaksvineyard.com

Hours: Thursday – Saturday, 8:00 a.m. to 6:00 p.m. (Central Time)
Groups, call to make sure she's there or to set an appointment
Wine Tasting: Free

If you visit Bridget Keegan, she will give you things. She may give you brochures, magazines, crackers, or apples, anything she has that she thinks you might like or can use, but most of all she will give you her wine. Generous by nature, if she has something, she will give it away, all part of her Golden Rule philosophy of life.

A second-generation Irish American, Bridget hails from Maryland where her Irish-born grandmother made whiskey during Prohibition, and taught her to make wine when she was a teenager. Bridget was also fond of growing things, so when she moved to Florida in the 1990s, she decided to grow fruit trees on 25 acres of land she

Some of Old Oaks Vineyard's award-winning wines

purchased near the small Panhandle town of Bonifay. She gradually added grape vines to the mix of peach and apple trees, planting the Florida hybrid grape Blanc du Bois and the Texas hybrid Champanel. She began making wine for family and friends who told their friends, and she soon had quite a following. In 2006, with no advertising or fanfare, she opened Old Oaks Vineyard.

"I opened as a small commercial winery and I've stayed that way," says Bridget. "I don't need a heart attack trying to grow a bigger business. I like it just the way it is. We're not Gallo."

The way it is allows Bridget to spend time talking with customers who visit the winery, as well as talking to area groups and organizations about growing grapes and making wine. She is active in the Florida Wine and Grape Growers' Association and in the American Wine Society. She also freely gives her time and advice to other winemakers who may be just starting out or who are looking for tips and tricks of the trade.

Old Oaks Vineyard is comprised of 25 acres at the winery site and another 20 acres at a farm nearby. In addition to the wine grapes, the vineyard grows pumpkins, watermelons, and peaches. In 2012, Old Oaks Vineyard was named a Certified Florida Farm Winery, producing just under 1000 cases of wine annually. With the help of family and friends, and anyone she can recruit, especially around harvest time, Bridget does all the work herself, from planting, to bottling, to pouring the finished product in her winery.

The wine production facility is located in the same small building as the tasting room, so visitors can see where all the wine magic takes place. Like a tireless leprechaun, Bridget takes you from one step in the process to the next, explaining how the pumpkin wine ages for a year and how all the wines have an average shelf-life of two years. The table wines are blended with 20% to 30% of other juices, Riesling from Ohio for the white and Malbec and sometimes Cabernet

Sauvignon from the west coast for the red. All the wines are made with Florida fruits.

Despite being tucked deep in the country down a dirt road, Bridget says she gets a lot of traffic from repeat customers and from people who have heard about her wines from others. She often has groups of military families visit, friends of friends who come taste her wine and enjoy the peace and quiet of the countryside. Sometimes, they buy wine, sometimes they don't, but for Bridget, that's okay. "It's all about giving what you can and treating people right."

Directions
From I-10, take exit 112 north onto State Road 79 to Bonifay. One mile north of Bonifay, turn left onto County Road 177 and go 5.4 miles. Turn right onto Will Lee Road (dirt road) and go 2.1 miles. Old Oaks Vineyard is on the left.

Bridget checks the temperature on one of the fermenting tanks in the winery.

Old Oaks Vineyard & Winery Wine List

All wines are subject to availability

White Table Wine – a blend of Blanc du Bois and Riesling; pairs well with fried foods, barbeque, salads, fish, cheeses, chocolate, and poultry

Red Table Wine – a blend of Champanel with Malbec and Cabernet Sauvignon; pairs well with mushrooms, pizza, barbeque, cheese, beef, fried foods, and turkey

Blanc du Bois – a refreshing white wine made from the Florida hybrid

*All of the following wines pair well with desserts, pastas, cheeses, vegetables, and cured meats

Pumpkin – a semi dry wine great for fall sipping

Peach – fresh fruit flavor in every sip

Watermelon – a light wine with a fresh from the field summer flavor

Diving in at Ponce de Leon Springs State Park

While you're here...

Old Oaks Vineyard & Winery is located in Holmes County, which is bordered on the north by Alabama, and has the Choctawhatchee River flowing through its middle. The county was created in 1848 with Bonifay as the county seat and offers some surprising historical attractions. U.S. Highway 90, originally the Old Spanish Road that once ran from St. Augustine to San Diego, California, runs through the south end of the county parallel to Interstate 10. The region is also an outdoor paradise with natural springs, lakes, creeks, and forests for plenty of outdoor activities.

Area Information
Holmes County Tourism Development
106 E. Byrd Avenue
Bonifay, Florida 32425
850-547-4682
www.holmescountyonline.com/tourism-development

Attractions – Note: All Opening Times are Central Time Zone
Holmes County Historical Society Museum
412 W. Kansas Avenue
Bonifay, Florida 32425
386-209-7936, Randy Torrance, President
www.holmescountyhistory.com
Open the second Saturday of each month from 10:00 a.m. to 2:00 p.m. The museum features artifacts and exhibits related to Holmes County history and early Florida rural life.

Keith Cabin
1320 County Road 179 (half mile south of State Road 2)
Bonifay, Florida 32425
www.keithcabinfoundation.org
This rare Louisiana Roof style log cabin with a wrap-around porch was built in 1886 and is Florida's only residential log home listed on the National Register of Historic Places.

Laura Ingalls Wilder Homestead
1225 Highway 163 (about ¾ mile north of State Road 2)
Westville, Florida 32464
www.hmdb.org/marker.asp?marker=95031
Historical marker and small park that commemorates the site of the 1891 Laura Ingalls Wilder home that she called the "little gray house in the piney woods."

Ponce de Leon Springs State Park
2860 State Park Road
Ponce de Leon Springs, Florida 32455
850-836-4281
www.floridastateparks.org/park/Ponce-de-Leon-Springs
Open daily 8:00 a.m. to sunset year round
Admission: $4 per vehicle, $2 pedestrians
Nature trails, a picnic area, and a natural spring pool that stays a cool 68°F are what draw visitors to this small Florida state park.

Fun Eats
Donut Land Express
1902 S. Waukesha Street
Bonifay, Florida 32425
850-547-2960
Homemade donuts and a great barbeque sandwich

Castaway Seafood
425 Saint Johns Road
Bonifay, Florida 32425
850-547-2112
Fried shrimp, fried oysters, hush puppies and coleslaw

Three Oaks Winery

Byron & Lucretia Biddle
3348 Highway 79
Vernon, Florida 32462
850-535-9463
www.threeoakswinery.com

Hours: Wednesday – Saturday, 9:30 a.m. to 5:00 p.m.
(Central Time)
Wine Tasting: Free

M aking wine wasn't Byron Biddle's first choice of occupation. A farmer by trade, Byron was very good at growing fruits and vegetables, which he did for years on land owned by his family for generations. Then, in 1989, Byron started growing grapes for other winemakers in the state, but soon decided that making wine was something he could do.

"I'd never made wine before," Byron explains. "But I was already growing the Conquistador grape and decided to give it a try."

He began making wine and people began buying it and wanting more of it, so in 1995 Three Oaks Winery became a state bonded winery. He soon realized that he needed someplace to sell his

wine other than his small production facility, so in 1996 he built a gift shop, the Grapevine, on Highway 79 south of the small village of Vernon (pop. 743). His wife Lucretia stocked the shop with gifts, candles, glassware, handmade clothing, books, baskets, antiques, and a large selection of Willow Tree Angels, and Byron stocked it with a selection of his wines.

Byron's original goal was to create fine wines from the Muscadine and hybrid grapes he grows in his vineyard as well as from Chardonnay and Merlot grapes he buys from vineyards outside the state. Since Three Oaks Winery is in a "dry county," the alcohol content of the wines is less than it is in many commercial wines, but Byron says that this is actually better for the grape, allowing more fruit flavor to emerge.

He began entering his wines in the annual Wine & Grape Juice Competition at the Florida State Fair and was soon bringing home medals. As the winemaker, Byron oversees the growing, harvest, and production of the wine grapes that he turns into his award-winning wines. Lucretia has amassed a vibrant collection of gift items in the gift shop that brings a steady stream of friends and neighbors looking for unique gifts and home décor items. Together, along with their children and grandchildren, the Biddles have created a solid family business. They have made Three Oaks Winery a certified Florida Farm Winery and a popular stop for travelers headed to and from the beach.

The winery has a total annual production of about 3000 gallons. The red wines are light and fruity and generally sweeter than European style wines. They range from a sweet dessert wine to a dry red and are made from the Florida hybrid bunch grape Conquistador, which is 40% Black Spanish and 20% Concord plus miscellaneous strains. Conquistador was developed by the University of Florida in 1983. Byron believes he is the only commercial winery in Florida growing and using the Conquistador grape and says these wines should be served chilled but not cold.

White wines include a semi-dry Chardonnay and a light, sweet wine made from the Carlos grape, a white variety of Muscadine grape. Also available is a non-alcoholic Muscadine grape juice. Clustered around the bottles of wine in the gift shop are the bronze, silver and gold medals these wines have won for excellence over the years.

Three Oaks Winery is open year-round and offers free winetasting of all their fine wines. Winery tours are available upon request.

Directions
From Interstate 10, take Exit 112 and go south on Highway 79 for about 10 miles to the town of Vernon. Stay on Highway 79 and go through town. As you leave town, the winery is on your right.

Three Oaks Winery Wine List

White Wines

Carlos - This sweet fruity white wine is made from the Carlos grape. It has a very smooth finish and a strong grape aroma and taste, a must for those who love the old fashioned flavor of the Muscadine grape. Serve chilled

Chardonnay – This traditional semi-dry Chardonnay is made from Chardonnay grapes crushed and fermented at Three Oaks Winery. Serve chilled

Red Wines

Merlot Sweet - This deliciously rich, sweet wine captures the flavor, fullness and robust qualities of this grape. Best served at room temperature

Merlot Semi-Dry - A slightly dry red wine, this one is perfect for those who are accustomed to a more traditional wine. Best served at room temperature

Conquistador Sweet Red – This is a slightly dryer red wine with a lighter Muscadine undertone.

Sweet Blueberry – Like freshly picked berries, this sweet blueberry dessert wine is perfect with fruit or flavorful desserts.

Conquistador Tawny Port – A gold medal winner at the 2011 International wine competition in Tampa, this port wine also has a higher alcohol content and is sold at shows outside Washington County between Thanksgiving and Christmas.

Blush Wines

Conquistador Vin Rosé – This wine is made in the traditional Rose' method of leaving the skins to ferment for a while and then removing them to maintain the blush color. Serve chilled

Non-Alcoholic Wines

Muscadine Grape Juice – This non-alcoholic, 100% Muscadine juice has no added sugar. Serve chilled

Moss Hill Church

While you're here...

Established in 1825, Washington County, named for George Washington, is an eco-tourism paradise. With the Choctawhatchee River on its western side and some of the highest limestone hills in the state on the east, the county is perfect for paddling and hiking. Vernon is named for Washington's home, Mount Vernon and was the county seat until 1927 when, by one vote, residents chose to move the seat of government to Chipley.

Area Information
Washington County Tourist Development Council
672 5th Street
Chipley, Florida 32428
850-638-6013
www.visitwcfla.com

Attractions – Note: All Opening Times are Central Time Zone
Moss Hill United Methodist Church
Take Moss Hill Road (Highway 279 south) out of Vernon for 3.6 miles to one of the oldest church buildings in Florida. Built around 1857 and still in use today, it is listed on the National Register of Historic Places. A marker tells the history of the church, and the cemetery holds the graves of veterans of the Indian Wars and the Civil War.

Falling Waters State Park
1130 State Park Road (off Highway 77 south of Interstate 10)
Chipley, Florida 32428
850-638-6130

www.floridastateparks.org/fallingwaters
Open daily 8:00 a.m. to sunset
Admission: $5 per vehicle
Full service RV and tent camping, hiking, swimming wildlife viewing, and picnicking on 171 acres. The park is on one of the highest hills in Florida and features Florida's highest waterfall.

Ebro Greyhound Park
6558 Dog Track Road (intersection of Highways 20 & 79)
Ebro, Florida 32437
850-234-3943
www.ebrogreyhoundpark.com
Open from mid-May through September of each year, Ebro Greyhound Park offers a complete schedule of greyhound racing, poker and poker tournaments and simulcasting from other tracks across the country.

Seacrest Wolf Preserve
3449 Bonnett Pond Road
Chipley, Florida 32428
850-773-2897
www.seacrestwolfpreserve.org
This non-profit wildlife organization provides a sanctuary for displaced captive wolves and offers educational programs about these beautiful animals. You can tour the facility by appointment. Seacrest also has full hook-up campsites for RVs and tents.

The Possum Monument
Located in downtown Wausau on State Road 77, and one of Florida's more unusual roadside attractions, the Possum Monument was erected to honor the "North American possum, a magnificent survivor of the marsupial family...furnishing both food and fur for the early settlers and their successors." Every year since 1982, the first Saturday in August has been Florida Possum Day and Wausau celebrates with the Possum Festival.

Bed & Breakfast
Choctaw Lodge Bed & Breakfast Retreat
781 Choctawhatchee River Road
Bruce, Florida 32455
850-835-1784
www.choctawlodgeretreat.com

Panama City Beach Winery

Larry & Kay Honeycutt
8730 Thomas Drive, Suite 1103B
Panama City Beach, Florida 32408
850-233-5950, 1-866-4WINERY (94-6379)
www.panamacitybeachwinery.com

Hours: Monday – Saturday, 10:00 a.m. to 5:00 p.m.
Sunday, noon to 5:00 p.m. (Central Time)
Wine Tasting: Free

When Larry Honeycutt uncorks a bottle of wine, it might be a dry blackberry, a tangy grapefruit, peach, carrot, kiwi, key lime, or even chocolate. While most wineries offer traditional wines made from grapes, Panama City Beach Winery offers 40 varieties of unique award-winning Florida fruit wines, sparkling wine, sherry and port that keep area residents and out-of-town tourists coming back for more.

Larry is the owner, greeter, wine pourer, and chief cheerleader of Panama City Beach Winery, and has been ever since he and his wife Kay opened the wine cellar in 2003. The retail wine and gift shop is an independently owned "satellite" store of Florida Orange

Groves Winery, a tropical fruit wine producer in St. Petersburg, Florida. The wines are made from 100% fruits.

"Wine can be made with anything that will ferment," says Larry," and Florida Orange Groves Winery makes exceptional wine from fruit other than grapes."

Although there is no onsite wine production facility, Panama City Beach Winery offers wine tasting and wine related gifts. The shop is a riot of color with dozens of whimsical wine bottle holders in the shapes of parrots, seagulls, fishermen, even Santa Claus. Wine glasses, bottle stoppers and wine accessories are available as are wine crackers, cheeses, sauces and Tortuga Caribbean Rum Cakes. They also carry Wind and Willow Cheese Ball and Dessert mixes and the Cool Freeze line of Wine Icee mixes that complement several of the wines.

At the back of the shop is a long tasting bar. Behind the bar, Larry shows off the dozens of wines draped in the medals they have won over the years in national and international competition, including Best of Show.

Listening to Larry talk about the wines, you see his eyes light up with excitement. "There are nine pounds of fruit in every bottle," he exclaims, "and the wine tastes like the juice it's made from. The tangerine tastes like tangerines and the blueberries taste like blueberries."

Larry says that about 40% of the people who come to his winery are not wine drinkers. "They come in and say, 'I don't really like wine.' Then I pour them a sample and they leave with six or eight bottles." He says his most popular wines are Mango Mamma and Category 5, a white sangria that is a blend of the most popular white wines.

All the wines are available for tasting. Larry says he doesn't sell anything that he doesn't sample. He says he usually starts by asking what fruits someone likes to get an idea of their tastes, then recommends certain wines from there.

The wine list sounds more like a salad bar; there are blueberry, blackberry, cherry, strawberry and peach wines. There are also carrot, tomato, honey, and watermelon wines. For dessert, there's chocolate, coconut, and key lime wines. The wines run from dry Muscadine to a sweet blackberry, so as Larry says, there's something for every taste, and he has a lot of tasters.

In fact, Larry says his winery is the most popular attraction in Panama City Beach and from the number of people tasting his wines and browsing his store, he may be right. Located across the street from the beach, the winery is a great place for people to get out of the heat and the sun, and swimsuits and shorts are acceptable attire.

Larry is proud of the fact that, according to Tripadvisor.com which lists 71 attractions for Panama City Beach, Panama City Beach Winery is number two with over 1100 reviews from all over the world. The reviews cite the friendly and personal service they get from Larry, and the delicious and unusual wines he sells. There's no mention of watching a tropical sunset with a glass of Panama City Beach Winery wine, but maybe there should be.

Directions
Panama City Beach Winery is on the east end of Panama City Beach. From U.S. Highway 98, take Front Beach Road to Thomas Drive. Go east on Thomas Drive to Joan Avenue. The winery is located in St. Thomas Square on the northeast corner of Joan Avenue and Thomas Drive.

Panama City Beach Winery Wine List

Florida Banana – Perfect for banana lovers, this wine goes well with pork, scallops or tilapia.

Black Gold – This dry blackberry wine goes great with veined cheese and red meat.

Black Gold (Sweet) – Made from a different variety of blackberries than Black Gold Dry, this lighter wine goes well with pasta and Italian dishes.

Blueberry Blue – Three pints of 100% Florida blueberries goes into every bottle of this semi-sweet wine that is perfect with steak.

Blueberry Blue Sparkling – A festive, bubbly version of blueberry wine.

40 Karat – This buttery semi-dry, white wine, similar to a Chardonnay, is made 100% from carrots and is excellent with shellfish and spicy foods.

Cherry Red – Not too dry, not too sweet, serve this cherry wine with steak, roast beef, burgers or desert.

Cocoa Beach – A blend of specialty orange juice and the richest chocolate gives this wine an explosion of chocolate flavor. Try it with Raspberry Mousse.

Coco Polada – This orange, pineapple and coconut wine delivers a "Jimmy Buffett" state of mind for lovers of piña coladas, and tropical sunsets.

Festiberry – A holiday wine that goes great with turkey, this wine has the crisp, fresh flavor of cranberry.

Florida Grapefruit – Made with 100% Florida pink grapefruit juice, this light, refreshing table wine is the perfect complement to seafood and salad.

Orange Blossom Honey – A mead made with Florida's orange blossom honey.

Key Limen – Nothing says Florida more than key lime and this wine captures the flavor of Key West on a balmy summer afternoon. Margarita lovers will love this one.

Mamma Guava – This tropical wine is an adventurous taste of pears, strawberries and pineapple with a lemon twist.

Mango Mamma – This semi-sweet to semi-dry tropical wine goes great with ham and mango kabobs or by the glass with a tropical sunset.

Mango Mamma Sparkling – A bubbly version of the Mango Mamma

Sinfully Noble – This dry Muscadine Vintner's reserve is a dark red wine made from the Muscadine Noble grape that radiates taste and aroma.

Sinfully Noble Semi-Sweet – A sweeter version of the Sinfully Noble dry wine

Orange Sunshine Dry – A pure orange juice wine, not a flavored wine product with an essence of orange. Makes a great salad dressing or marinade base.

Orange Sunshine Semi-Sweet – A sweeter version of the Orange Sunshine dry

Midnight Sun – The Orange Sunshine Wine is aged with fresh roasted coffee beans creating a real flavor treat. This is an excellent brunch or desert wine.

Florida Fever – Made with passion fruit, this wine is tart and flavorful and will enhance any meal. Great poolside or sitting on the beach.

White Gold – A true southern delight, this peach wine is great with barbecue or serve it over ice cream.

Sunset Pineapple – Capture the tropical flavor of the Hawaiian Islands with pineapple wine. Makes a great fruit salad base or goes well when serving ham.

Eleganta – This rich flavorful red raspberry wine adds a special touch to any occasion. Serve with cheesecake or dark chocolate.

Category "5" – A refreshing white sangria derived from a blend of white fruit wines.

Strawberry Blush – Made with fresh Florida strawberries, this blush wine is great with sandwiches, salads, and desert and a real surprise with spaghetti.

Tangelo – Made with juice from the Florida Honeybell, a cross between the Dancy Tangerine and the Duncan Grapefruit. Wonderfully light and refreshing, this wine is also a great complement to any seafood dish.

Tangier – A specialty wine for tangerine lovers with a powerful bouquet of honey, citrus, and flowers

Hot Sun – A very smooth dry white wine with a hint of tomato and peppers that will spice up any Mexican dish, or serve with oysters.

Watermelon – Bring back the lazy days of summer with this wonderfully light, sweet wine. Pack with your next picnic or serve at your next barbecue.

Cracker Hammock Crackle - This grapefruit sparkling wine will add sparkle to any party, bridal shower, or get together. For a delightful addition, float fresh strawberries in each glass.

Cracker Hammock Crackle - A tangerine sparkling wine that will add sparkle to a lobster or crab dinner.

Millennium Gold – A combination of strawberry wine and four year old oak-aged brandy that is then aged for an additional two years makes this strawberry cream sherry a hit with sherry lovers.

Dolphin Show at Gulf World Marine Park

While you're here...

Panama City Beach is one of Florida's most popular beaches. Once known for its Spring Break crowds of college kids, the Beach today offers a broad range of theme parks, restaurants, shopping, and activities for families, couples, and friend getaways. From championship golf courses, to world class resorts and spas, to wine and music events, there's a lot to do in PCB.

Area Information
Panama City Beach Convention and Visitors' Bureau
17001 Panama City Beach Parkway (U.S. Highway 98)
Panama City Beach, Florida 32413
1-800-PCBEACH (722-3224)
www.visitpanamacitybeach.com

Attractions– Note: All Opening Times are Central Time Zone
Gulf World Marine Park
15412 Front Beach Road
Panama City Beach, Florida 32413
850-234-5271
www.gulfworldmarinepark.com
Open daily from 9:30 a.m. to 4:30 p.m.
Admission: $29 Adults, $14 Children 5 to 11, Children under 5 free ($5 savings per ticket for booking online) Additional pricing for special programs
Dolphin shows, sea lion shows, and interactive programs give this iconic theme park a variety of activities.

Science & Discovery Center
308 Airport Road
Panama City, Florida 32405
850-769-6128
www.scienceanddiscoverycenter.org
Open Tuesday – Saturday, 10:00 a.m. to 5:00 p.m.
Admission: $7 Adults, $6 Seniors, Children & Military
This hands-on science and nature museum has activities in electricity, light and color, and the human body, and has a pioneer village, a reptile room, and a nature trail.

Shipwreck Island Water Park
12201 Hutchison Boulevard
Panama City Beach, Florida 32407
850-234-3333
www.shipwreckisland.com
Open daily June to the first week in August, limited opening April, May and the rest of August
Admission: $35.98 plus tax above 50 inches tall, $29.98 plus tax below 50 inches tall, Children below 35 inches tall admitted free
This 20-acre waterpark with a tropical theme has a 500,000-gallon ocean motion wave pool, river rapids ride, a lazy river ride, and a 65-foot platform from which two slides drop.

St. Andrews State Park
4607 State Park Lane
Panama City Beach, Florida 32408
850-708-6100
www.floridastateparks.org/StAndrews
Open daily 8:00 a.m. to sunset
Admission: $8 per vehicle, additional fees for camping and boat launching
In 1995, St. Andrews was named best beach in America by Dr. Beach. This 1,260-acre state park has over a mile of pure white sand beaches camping, hiking, fishing, boating, and an alligator lagoon.

Ripley's Believe It or Not! Museum
9907 Front Beach Road
Panama City Beach, Florida 32407
850-230-6113
www.ripleys.com/panamacitybeach

Open daily 9:00 a.m. to 10:00 p.m.
Admission: $17.99 Adults, $12.99 Children aged 5 to 12, Children under 5 free, Additional pricing for Moving Theater
This long time PBC attraction exhibits oddities from around the world and has a 4D Moving Theater and an interactive laser room.

Nivol Brewery
473 N. Richard Jackson Boulevard
Panama City Beach, Florida 32407
850-249-1150
www.nivolbrewery.com
Open Sunday – Thursday, 2:00 p.m. to 9:00 p.m.
Friday & Saturday, 2:00 p.m. to midnight
Microbrewery and tap room featuring craft beer tours and tastings, WiFi and pet friendly

Bed & Breakfast
Wisteria Inn
20404 Front Beach Road
Panama City Beach, Florida 32413
850-234-0557
www.wisteria-inn.com

Fun Eats
Capt. Anderson's Restaurant
5551 N. Lagoon Drive
Panama City Beach, Florida 32408
850-234-2225
www.captanderson.com
Open February through mid-November and serving dinner only, this family owned award-winning waterfront restaurant is a Panama City Beach icon.

Hammerhead Fred's
8752 Thomas Drive
Panama City Beach, Florida 32408
850-233-3907
www.hammerheadfreds.com
Fun, funky, and very casual, this is the place to fill up on fresh seafood and Apalachicola oysters.

Sharky's Beachfront Restaurant & Tiki Bar
15201 Front Beach Road
Panama City Beach, Florida 32413
850-235-2420
www.sharkysbeach.com
A beachfront restaurant with live music, a children's playground and miles of sand serving seafood, sandwiches, and salads

Shopping
Pier Park
16000 Front Beach Road
Panama City Beach, Florida 32413
850-236-9974 Mall Information
This mall on the beach features retail stores, restaurants, and entertainment, including Guy Harvey's Island Grill, Jimmy Buffet's Margaritaville, Dillard's, Hollister, Ron Jon Surf Shop, and more.

Mr. Surf's Surf Shop
7220 Thomas Drive
Panama City Beach, Florida 32408
850-235-2702 or Surf Report Line 850-235-2217
Supplying bikinis, boards, and beach gear since 1982

White sand and blue-green water are the trademarks of Panama City Beach.

Emerald Coast Wine Cellars

1708 Scenic Gulf Drive, Suite C
Miramar Beach, Florida 32550
850-837-9500
www.emeraldcoastwinecellars.com

Hours: Daily 10:00 a.m. to 6:00 p.m. (Central Time)
Wine Tasting: Free

Just steps away from the sugar-white sands and the blue-green waters of the Gulf of Mexico is a treasure chest full of wine, gourmet foods and gifts. Opened in 2001 as a way to offer Chautauqua wines to beachgoers, Emerald Coast Wine Cellars is a sister business to Chautauqua Vineyards & Winery located about 35 miles north in DeFuniak Springs (see page 155). As a bonded winery, Emerald Coast Wine Cellars offers complimentary wine tastings, gift shopping and made-to-order gift baskets.

Located across the street from the beach, Emerald Coast Wine Cellars is very beach-casual, and beach apparel is perfectly acceptable attire (shirts and shoes, please). You can browse in air-conditioned comfort and the wine shop personnel are happy to pour wine and help you with wine and gift selections.

"We offer the same wines as Chautauqua Vineyards with the same labels," says manager Melissa Webster. At first glance, this might seem confusing but Melissa explains it. All Muscadine wines have the Chautauqua label and all other wines carry the Emerald label.

Stepping into Emerald Coast Wine Cellars you're immediately confronted with a tantalizing array of wines and specialty food items. In addition to making wine, Chautauqua Vineyards makes sauces, salsas, jams and jellies. There are also nuts and snacks, gourmet chocolates, decorated cookies and racks filled with 18 different wines. Then there are the wine accessories; wine glasses, wine racks, wine stoppers, corkscrews, cocktail napkins even tee-shirts with sayings like "Wine Diva" and "I only serve the finest wines, did you bring any?"

A major part of Emerald Coast Wine Cellars' business is custom made gift baskets. Upstairs there are special sections devoted to brides, babies, "gifts for her" such as spa items, soaps and candles, Christmas ornaments, and everything beachy. Gift baskets are made onsite and can be delivered locally or shipped.

Complimentary wine tasting is offered at the wine bar with wines ranging from a dry Chardonnay and Merlot to sweet dessert wines that include a Vanilla Sherry and a Chocolate Port, special creations of Chautauqua Vineyards.

Emerald Coast Wine Cellars Tasting Room

The Muscadine grapes for Chautauqua wines are grown on Chautauqua Vineyards' 40 acres in north Walton County. Chardonnay, Merlot and Cabernet wines are made from juices or grapes brought in from other regions. Harvest and crush take place at Chautauqua Winery in August through September and visitors may watch the process and learn about winemaking. For anyone who's never seen a Muscadine vine, Emerald Coast Wine Cellars has one growing outside on the front porch, a testament to the hardiness of these native grapes.

Chautauqua wines are sold exclusively at Emerald Coast Wine Cellars and at Chautauqua Vineyards & Winery in DeFuniak Springs.

Directions
Take U.S. Highway 98 to Miramar Beach in Walton County. At Silver Sands Factory Outlet, turn south onto Scenic Gulf Drive (CR 2378) and travel 1.7 miles. The winery is on your right.

Emerald Coast Wine Cellars Wine List

Note: Chautauqua Vineyards is the parent company and makes all the wines for Emerald Coast Wine Cellars and Chautauqua Winery. The wine list below is the same for both businesses.

Red Wines

Merlot – This dry red table wine is a classic Merlot with full fruit flavor and a smooth finish.

Noble – This semi-sweet red Muscadine wine is made from Noble grapes that are crushed and fermented with the skins on to extract the full fruit flavor.

Sunset Red – This semi-sweet red table wine made from Concord grapes is versatile as a summer sipping wine or as a hot mulled wine in winter.

White Wines

Chardonnay – This classic dry white table wine has a harmony of fruit and oak and a perfect balance of ripe fruit and firm acid.

Carlos – This award-winning semi-sweet white Muscadine wine is made from Carlos grapes and fermented at low temperatures to capture the luscious flavor and aroma of the fruit.

Sugar Sands White – This semi-sweet white wine is made from fragrant Niagara Muscadine grapes.

Wild Honey Flower – This sweet white Muscadine wine made from Carlos grapes and sweetened with wildflower honey is reminiscent of late-harvest style wines with rich aroma and full, round finish.

Blush & Sparkling Wines

Blush –A blend of Carlos and Noble Muscadine grapes gives this wine a rich blush color and a semi-sweet finish.

Fruit Wines and Blends

Beachberry – A casual wine made from infusing natural peach and orange flavors into premium table wine, Beachberry finishes sweet to complement the round flavor of the peach and orange blend.

Winterberry – This seasonal wine is made from cranberry juice, natural spices and natural mulled wine flavors for a mid-winter holiday treat.

Blueberry – This popular sweet blueberry wine is made from pure Southern blueberries.

Blackberry – Made from select blackberries picked at the peak of their flavor and intensity, this wine finishes sweet and flavorful.

Fortified Wines
Sherry – This classic American sherry has a rich, nutty bouquet that complements the creamy texture. Made from Carlos grapes, the wine is baked and aged in barrels to achieve its complexity.

Port – A classic dessert wine made from Noble grapes, this wine is aged in wooden barrels to give it a depth of flavor, aroma and complexity that only comes with time.

Vanilla Sherry – This unique dessert wine is made by adding a Madagascar bourbon vanilla bean to the premium cream sherry before corking and sealing. The wine is then flavored and infused during bottle aging with the luscious aroma and tropical flavor of pure vanilla.

Chocolate Port – Crafted from the best port and a select blend of cacao beans, the wine is bottled and the beans added before corking to produce a rich, dark, earthy chocolate bouquet and flavor.

The Wesley House at Eden Gardens State Park

While you're here...

South Walton is known for its snow-white beach sands and turquoise-colored gulf waters, rare coastal dune lakes and great dining (Chef Emeril Lagasse lives here). It is also home to the largest designer outlet center in the country, Sandestin Golf and Beach Resort, and to the "new urbanism" of Seaside, WaterColor, and Rosemary Beach. Hiking, biking, beachcombing, shopping, and eating are a normal day's activities in SoWal.

Area Information
South Walton Tourist Development Council
25777 U.S. Highway 331 South
Santa Rosa Beach, Florida 32459
1-800-822-6877 or 850-267-1216
www.visitsouthwalton.com

Attractions – Note: All Opening Times are Central Time Zone
Village of Baytowne Wharf
9300 Emerald Coast Parkway (U.S. Highway 98)
Sandestin Golf and Beach Resort
Miramar Beach, Florida 32550
850-267-8180
www.baytownewharf.com
Located on the Sandestin resort property, the Village has entertainment for both kids and adults and includes unique stores, a variety of restaurants, live music and shows, a kid-friendly zip line, a climbing wall, and 40-foot tall rappelling tower.

Eden Gardens State Park
181 Eden Gardens Road (off County Road 395 North)
Santa Rosa Beach, Florida 32459
850-267-8320
www.floridastateparks.org/park/Eden-Gardens
Open daily 8:00 a.m. to sunset, Guided Tours of the Wesley House are
Thursday - Monday, 10:00 a.m. to 3:00 p.m. hourly
Admission: $4 per vehicle. House Tours: $4 Adult, $2 Children
This 161-acre state park on Tucker Bayou features a fully-furnished
historic home with the second largest collection of Louis XVI furniture
in the country. There are gardens with azaleas, camellias and ancient
oaks, a nature trail, and a picnic area.

Bed & Breakfast
Hibiscus Coffee & Guesthouse
85 DeFuniak Street (Grayton Beach)
Santa Rosa Beach, Florida, 32459
850-231-2733 - www.hibiscusflorida.com

Lisbeth's Bed & Breakfast by the Sea
3501 E. County Hwy 30A
Santa Rosa Beach, Florida 32459
850-231-1577 - www.lisbethsbb.com

Fun Eats
The Whale's Tail Beach Bar & Grill
1373 Scenic Gulf Drive
Miramar Beach, Florida 32550
850-650-4377
www.seascape-resort.com/the-whales-tail-destin
This beachside eatery serves breakfast, lunch, and dinner and features
sandwiches, salads, and fresh seafood. It's one of the few places you
can eat right on the beach.

Pompano Joe's Seafood House
2237 Scenic Gulf Drive
Miramar Beach, Florida 32550
850-837-2224 - www.pompano-joes.com
Fun, funky, and colorful, this Caribbean flavored beachfront
restaurant features Jamaican jerk chicken, fresh seafood, and a
beachside bar.

Shopping

Silver Sands Factory Stores
10562 Emerald Coast Parkway (U.S. Highway 98)
Miramar Beach, Florida 32550
850-654-9771
www.premiumoutlets.com/outlet/silver-sands
The largest designer outlet mall in the country with over 100 brand
name stores plus restaurants and specialty foods.

Grand Boulevard Town Center at Sandestin
U.S. Highway 98, just east of the entrance to Sandestin
Miramar Beach, Florida 32550
850-837-3099
www.grandboulevard.com
Shopping and dining options here include Mitchell's Fish Market,
Tommy Bahama's Restaurant & Bar, and Emeril's Coastal Italian.

*The Gulf Coast beaches of South Walton and Destin are famous for their white sand and
turquoise-colored water.*

Chautauqua Vineyards & Winery

364 Hugh Adams Road
DeFuniak Springs, Florida 32435
850-892-5887
www.chautauquawinery.com

Hours: Daily 9:00 a.m. to 5:00 p.m. (Central Time)
Wine Tasting: Free

Old vines make great wines, or so the saying goes. Making wines from vines planted in the 1970s has certainly been rewarding for Chautauqua Vineyards & Winery, as the number of medals won by their wines would indicate. A certified Florida Farm Winery and one of Florida's oldest wineries, Chautauqua Vineyards' estate wines reflect the origins of America's wine industry, which began some 450 years ago and 350 miles to the east.

The name Chautauqua comes from the Florida Chautauqua Center, the arts, education and cultural association that makes its home in DeFuniak Springs. The vineyard grows Muscadine grapes on 40 acres north of DeFuniak Springs. Hearty and native to Florida and the southeast, Muscadine vines resist some of the usual pests and problems associated with European varieties. The grapes are also sweeter by nature but offer a range of possibilities for winemakers like George Cowie.

Born into a family of winemakers, George grew up tending vines and making wines at his family's estate winery, Cowie Wine Cellars and Vineyards in Paris, Arkansas. When he moved from Paris to DeFuniak Springs in 1990 to become Chautauqua Vineyard's winemaker, he knew he had a big job ahead of him.

The winery opened with its first vintage in 1989. When George came on board, there wasn't yet a Chautauqua wine image, which could have been a daunting task for a young man just out of college. However, George was armed with a Bachelor's degree and a Master's degree in Food Science from the University of Arkansas. While there, he worked both as an undergraduate and in graduate school for renowned viticulture and oenology expert Dr. Justin Morris in a research group, and his Master's thesis was on the effect of canopy management on juice and wine quality. George was up to the task. In the more than 20 years since that time George has put his mark on the wines, creating some distinctive and original flavors.

"The estate wines are made from two traditional Muscadine grapes, Carlos and Noble," says George. "We also make dessert wines, sherry and port, from these grapes and have been having some fun with different flavors. It's something interesting to play with."

Something to play with, indeed. George and his crew have experimented with pure Madagascar bourbon vanilla beans and a select blend of pure cacao beans to create a flavorful vanilla sherry and a dark, earthy chocolate port. George says they are both interesting wines that hold their own at the dessert table.

Stainless steel tanks are used to ferment the wines.

Other Chautauqua wines include Noble and Carlos, several blends, fruit wines such as blueberry and blackberry, and a sparkling wine. They also make Chardonnay, Merlot, and Cabernet Sauvignon wines from grapes trucked in from the north or from fresh juices.

Chautauqua Vineyards & Winery has a 75,000-gallon capacity and produces about 10,000 to 11,000 cases of wine annually. With their Europress, a custom-built wine press that is the largest press of its kind east of the Rockies, they also do custom crushing for other vineyards and make wines for private labels. Chautauqua wines are produced under two labels, Chautauqua for the Muscadine wines and Emerald for other wines.

Emerald refers to Emerald Coast Wine Cellars, Chautauqua's sister winery located in Miramar Beach, about 35 miles south of DeFuniak Springs on the gulf coast (see page 147). The two wineries have created a working relationship that suits the capabilities of both locations. Chautauqua Vineyards makes all the wines for both wineries and Emerald Coast Wine Cellars makes all of the gift baskets.

Like Emerald Coast, Chautauqua Vineyards & Winery has a well-stocked gift and wine shop, although not as extensive. You will find glasses, cocktail napkins, coasters, wine racks and wine accessories, tee-shirts ("Wine a Little, You'll Feel Better) as well as licensed team items for Florida State University and other colleges. You'll also find all of the wines Chautauqua Vineyards makes. A complimentary wine tasting bar allows visitors to relax and taste the wines at their leisure.

Down the hall, a separate room overlooking the stainless steel fermenting tanks gives visitors a bird's-eye view of the production facilities and displays old photos of DeFuniak Springs as well as the many awards and ribbons Chautauqua wines have won at national and international wine competitions. A video shows the winemaking process from vines to bottle, including harvest, crush, and fermentation. This is all part of the complimentary winery tour. During harvest (August to September) visitors can see the grapes arriving at the winery and going through crush.

After 21 years as winemaker, George Cowie has high praise for everyone involved with Chautauqua Vineyards & Winery, from owner Paul Owens to general manager Steve White and all the staff. Most of the employees have been there 15 to 20 years or more and George thinks that says a lot about the organization.

"It's good people making good wines with good value and local flavor," he says.

Directions
Take Exit 85 off I-10 and go north to the first traffic light. Turn right, then right again onto Hugh Adams Road. Follow the road around to the winery.

Chautauqua Vineyards & Winery
Wine List

Note: Chautauqua Vineyards is the parent company and makes all the wines for Chautauqua Winery and Emerald Coast Wine Cellars. The wine list below is the same for both businesses.

Red Wines

Merlot – This dry red table wine is a classic Merlot with full fruit flavor and a smooth finish.

Noble – This semi-sweet red Muscadine wine is made from Noble grapes that are crushed and fermented with the skins on to extract the full fruit flavor.

Sunset Red – This semi-sweet red table wine made from Concord grapes is versatile as a summer sipping wine or as a hot mulled wine in winter.

White Wines

Chardonnay – This classic dry white table wine has a harmony of fruit and oak and a perfect balance of ripe fruit and firm acid.

Carlos – This award-winning semi-sweet white Muscadine wine is made from Carlos grapes and fermented at low temperatures to capture the luscious flavor and aroma of the fruit.

Sugar Sands White – This semi-sweet white wine is made from fragrant Niagara Muscadine grapes.

Wild Honey Flower – This sweet white Muscadine wine made from Carlos grapes and sweetened with wildflower honey is reminiscent of late-harvest style wines with rich aroma and full, round finish.

Blush & Sparkling Wines

Blush –A blend of Carlos and Noble Muscadine grapes gives this wine a rich blush color and a semi-sweet finish.

Fruit Wines and Blends

Beachberry – A casual wine made from infusing natural peach and orange flavors into premium table wine, Beachberry finishes sweet to complement the round flavor of the peach and orange blend.

Winterberry – This seasonal wine is made from cranberry juice, natural spices and natural mulled wine flavors for a mid-winter holiday treat.

Blueberry – This popular sweet blueberry wine is made from pure Southern blueberries.

Blackberry – Made from select blackberries picked at the peak of their flavor and intensity, this wine finishes sweet and flavorful.

Fortified Wines
Sherry – This classic American sherry has a rich, nutty bouquet that complements the creamy texture. Made from Carlos grapes, the wine is baked and aged in barrels to achieve its complexity.

Port – A classic dessert wine made from Noble grapes, this wine is aged in wooden barrels to give it a depth of flavor, aroma and complexity that only comes with time.

Vanilla Sherry – This unique dessert wine is made by adding a Madagascar bourbon vanilla bean to the premium cream sherry before corking and sealing. The wine is then flavored and infused during bottle aging with the luscious aroma and tropical flavor of pure vanilla.

Chocolate Port – Crafted from the best port and a select blend of cacao beans, the wine is bottled and the beans added before corking to produce a rich, dark, earthy chocolate bouquet and flavor.

Chautauqua Brotherhood Hall in DeFuniak Springs

While you're here...

The history of DeFuniak Springs involves a round lake, a railroad magnate, and a New York cultural organization looking for a new home. The round lake, a rare natural phenomenon, still is the centerpiece of this historically significant Florida town. When in the 1880s, officials of the Pensacola & Atlantic Railroad were looking for a place to create a resort for wealthy northerners, they decided this was the perfect spot. The New York Chautauqua society, an education and arts organization, got on board, and the town was born. Today, the annual Chautauqua Festival in January brings visitors from all over the world for live performances and cultural studies.

Area Information
South Walton Tourist Development Council
25777 U.S. Highway 331 South
Santa Rosa Beach, Florida 32459
1-800-822-6877
www.visitsouthwalton.com

Attractions – Note: All Opening Times are Central Time Zone
Historic Downtown DeFuniak Springs
DeFuniak Springs was named for Frederick R. De Funiak, a vice-president of the L&N Railroad, the parent company of the Pensacola and Atlantic line. The town's visitor center is located next to the old L&N caboose across from Lake DeFuniak and you can get information there. A walk or drive around the lake is a must to see the stately homes and historic buildings. The Chautauqua Brotherhood Hall is located here, as is the oldest continuously-in-use library in Florida.

Walton County Heritage Association Museum
1140 Circle Drive
DeFuniak Springs, Florida 32435
850-951-2127
www.waltoncountyheritage.org
Open Tuesday – Saturday, 1:00 p.m. to 4:00 p.m.
Admission: Free
This small historical museum is housed in the old train depot with exhibits and artifacts related to local history.

DeFuniak Springs Art Co-op
782 Baldwin Avenue
DeFuniak Springs, Florida 32435
850-419-3007
www.facebook.com/defuniakspringsartcoop
Open Monday – Friday, 10:00 a.m. to 5:00 p.m.
Saturday, 10:00 a.m. to 4:00 p.m.
Gallery displaying the works of local artists in a variety of media.

Morrison Springs
874 Morrison Springs Road (off County Road 181)
Ponce de Leon, Florida 32455
850-892-8108
Open daily, sunrise to sunset
Admission: Free
This 161-acre county maintained park is a popular swimming, diving and picnicking spot and is known to divers from all over the world. The focal point of the park is a 250-foot diameter spring pool that produces an estimated 70 million gallons of water per day.

Fun Eats
Bogey's Bar & Restaurant
660 Baldwin Avenue
DeFuniak Springs, Florida 32433
850-951-2233
www.bogeysrestaurant.net
Serving lunch and dinner (and take-out), Bogey's features an eclectic menu with everything from almond encrusted baked brie to a Filet Mignon with Portobello mushrooms. The upper deck has a view of the lake.

H & M Hot Dog

43 S. 9th Street
DeFuniak Springs, Florida 32433
850-892-9100
It may not be much to look at, but locals say it's the best place to get a burger or a Chicago-style hot dog. Open since 1947, H & M is the oldest continuously operating hot dog stand in Florida.

Shopping

Nook and Cranny

676 Baldwin Avenue
DeFuniak Springs, Florida 32433
850-865-2976
Consignment store featuring furniture, antiques, and collectibles

The Little Big Store

35 S. 8th Street
DeFuniak Springs, Florida 32433
850-892-6066
Old-fashioned general store featuring kitchen items, sodas, candy, tea pots, yoyos books, locally made soaps, and a gazillion other items.

The Little Big Store carries everything from toys to kitchenware.

"*A meal without wine*
is like a day without sunshine."

- Louis Pasteur (1822-1895)
French biologist and chemist

De Luna Wines

Steve Brown, Bethany Wilson, Carl Wilson
116 E. Gonzalez Street
Pensacola, Florida 32501
850-332-6341
www.deluna.com

Tasting Room opening Fall 2017
Call for opening hours

Spanish explorers in the 16th Century probably didn't stop long enough in their travels to make wine, but they certainly enjoyed drinking it whenever they had the chance. Unfortunately for them, it was a long trip back to Spain when they ran out, so barrels of wine were generally part of their essential provisions aboard ship.

Now, 500 years later, you'll find the name of one of those explorers on bottles of some of Florida's newest wine. Since 2014, De Luna Wines have been steadily making their way into stores and wine shops from Pensacola to Key West, invoking the name of Tristan de Luna, who established Pensacola as the first European colony in the New World in 1559.

Billed as America's First Craft Cocktail Wine! ™ De Luna wines are fruit-filled and fun. The brain-child of Steve Brown, long-time Pensacola entrepreneur and wine lover, the business started out differently than most wineries, some might even say backwards, but that's not what Steve thought.

"My Dad said, we will not start this journey unless we have distribution," says Bethany Wilson, Steve's daughter and the National Marketing Director for De Luna Wines. "He believed that if we were going to make a go of the business for the long term, we had to start with distribution and the winery would come later." So, that's just what they did.

The journey began with Bethany and Carl's wedding. Wanting a small, family affair, Bethany's only request was that Steve make some of his delicious homemade strawberry wine that he often made for holidays and as gifts. He made a batch for the wedding and friends and family raved about it, telling Steve he needed to sell it.

Steve began making wine and selling it locally. Then Bethany started traveling, driving her car all over the state and stopping into liquor stores and grocery stores, where ever she found wine being sold. Soon Carl, with a background in organic chemistry, stepped in to help make the wine and De Luna Wines became a full-fledged family business. Today, De Luna Wines can be found in Walgreens, Total Wine, Wal-Mart, Sam's Clubs, and countless grocery stores and ABC Liquors the length and breadth of the state.

With distribution increasing, they soon found they needed more research and production space. They knew they wanted to be downtown and searched until they found a 17,000 square-foot facility in the North Hill Historical District. The surrounding lot takes up most of the city block Although the building was leased, they bought it in December 2016 and moved into the available space until the lease was up. Once part of the Cary and Company coal yard, the property holds both historical significance and some intriguing design elements.

"See how that wall goes at an angle," says Bethany. "We're going to make it look like a pirate ship, and there'll be an underground cave and lots of wine barrels." Her eyes light up with the vision of what will essentially be a wine theme park. "We'll have an outdoor courtyard here with a fountain splashing and lights twinkling overhead, and we'll do winery tours and have a wedding venue."

The ideas just keep coming, and they include the wine bottles and the whole De Luna theme. Ancient mariners were superstitious and myths of mermaids and other sea creatures were common. In addition, ships were often in danger of attack by pirates who hid in bays and coves along the coast hoping to score treasure from an unsuspecting explorer. With the current popularity of both mermaids and pirates, Bethany says it was a natural move to incorporate them into De Luna Wine's marketing campaign.

"We have fun wines and we thought, why not have some fun and put mermaids and pirates on the labels?" says Bethany. As a result, the labels have garnered a lot of attention, both on store shelves and at festivals and special events that they attend.

As for the wines themselves, Bethany says they wanted to introduce something new and different into the market. Smooth and semi-sweet, all the wines pair well with most meats, cheeses, pastas, and particularly with chocolate. Bethany calls them party wines, and they've developed cocktail recipes with names like De Luna Delirium (blueberry wine and vodka), De Luna's Hurricane (pomegranate wine, rum, peach schnapps, and pineapple juice), and Beached Mermaid (cherry wine, jagermeister, and peach schnapps).

Steve stands atop pallets of De Luna wine ready for shipping.

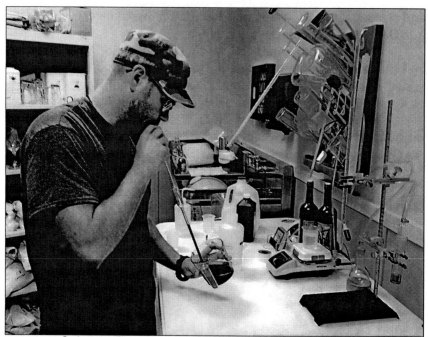
Carl researches and tests at all phases of the winemaking process.

De Luna Wine buys juice directly from farmers and all processing, fermentation, and bottling takes place onsite. Current annual production is roughly 65,000 gallons, but that is constantly increasing to meet distributor demand. De Luna's production capacity is 15,000 gallons and it takes 60 days to make a batch of wine.

Construction of the winery and its pirates and mermaids themed attractions began in October 2017. Phase I includes the tasting room, the pirate ship façade, and the front courtyard. As of this writing, a grand opening is set for late October, but visitors are advised to call ahead to make sure the winery is open.

With distribution well established, Bethany says De Luna can now concentrate on the next step. "We want to build the most beautiful winery you could possibly imagine!"

Directions
Take Interstate 10 to Interstate 110 south. Take exit 2 and turn right onto East Cervantes Street. Go two blocks and turn right onto North Palafox Street. Go two blocks and turn right onto East Gonzales Street De Luna Wine is in the second block on the left across from First City Art Center.

De Luna Wines Wine List

*Great on their own, paired with food, or mixed
as cocktails*

Cherry Bomb – Michigan-grown Montmorency cherries give this wine a blast of flavor

Strawberry Kiwi Splash – Bold Southern style in a classic strawberry wine

Blueberry Explosion – This blueberry wine is bursting with fresh blueberry flavor

Pomegranate Pop – A fresh and spirited twist on this ancient fruit

National Naval Aviation Museum

While you're here...

Historic Pensacola is a city brimming with modern amenities and is a great vacation destination. The area offers historic sites, museums, restaurants, shopping, and outdoor activities, and is only minutes to the beach. There are several state parks close by and the Gulf Islands National Seashore offers swimming, picnicking, and hiking as well as the chance to explore historic Fort Pickens.

Area Information
Visit Pensacola Visitor Center
1401 E. Gregory Street
Pensacola, Florida 32561
1-800-874-1234   - www.visitpensacola.com

Attractions – Note: All Opening Times are Central Time Zone
National Naval Aviation Museum
1750 Radford Boulevard, Suite C
Naval Air Station Pensacola, Florida 32508
850-452-3604 or 850-452-3606
www.navalaviationmuseum.org
Open daily 9:00 a.m. to 5:00 p.m. (allow yourself 2 or 3 hours)
Admission: Free
Home of the Blue Angels, this one of the most visited museums in the southeast. Aircraft exhibits, a giant screen theater, flight simulators, and a chance to watch the Blue Angels practice are just some of the things to do here. You can also explore nearby Fort Barrancas and the Pensacola Lighthouse.

First City Art Center
1060 N. Guillemard Street
Pensacola, Florida 32501
850-429-1222
www.firstcityart.org
Across the street from De Luna Winery, watch artists at work, or take a class. There are demonstrations of glassblowing and ceramics, and a gallery that features work from local artists in a variety of media.

T. T. Wentworth Museum and Historic Pensacola Village
120 Church Street
Pensacola, Florida 32502
850-595-5985
www.historicpensacola.org
Open Tuesday – Saturday, 10:00 a.m. to 4:00 p.m.
Admission: $8 adults 15 years and older, $4 children ages 3 to 14
This complex of museums, restored and furnished houses and buildings, costumed interpreters, and a Colonial Archaeological Trail tells the history of Pensacola.

Veteran's Memorial Park
E. Romana Street and Bayfront Parkway
Pensacola, Florida 32502
850-434-6119
veteransmemorialparkpensacola.com
Open daily, sunrise to sunset
Admission: Free
Honoring all branches of the military, the park includes paved walkways, gardens, and the "Wall South," the only permanent replica of the National Vietnam Memorial.

Pensacola Museum of Art
407 S. Jefferson Street
Pensacola, Florida 32502
850-432-6247
www.pensacolamuseum.org
Open Tuesday – Wednesday, 10:00 a.m. to 5:00 p.m., Thursday – Saturday, 10:00 a.m. to 7:00 p.m., Sunday, noon to 4:00 p.m.
Admission: $8 adults 15 years and older, $4 children ages 3 to 14
Housed in the old city jail, the museum features a permanent collection of modern and contemporary art and temporary exhibits.

Bed & Breakfast
Noble Manor Bed & Breakfast
110 W. Strong Street
Pensacola, Florida 32501
850-434-9544
www.noblemanor.com

Pensacola Victorian
203 W. Gregory Street
Pensacola, Florida 32501
850-434-2818
www.pensacolavictorian.com

Fun Eats
The Fish House
600 S. Barracks Street
Pensacola, Florida 32501
850-470-0003
www.fishhousepensacola.com
Seafood, drinks and great desserts overlooking Pensacola Bay. Try the shrimp and grits.

Five Sisters Blues Cafe
421 W. Belmont Street
Pensacola, Florida 32501
850-912-4856
www.fivesistersbluescafe.com
Soul food in the downtown historic district, serving meatloaf, fried green tomatoes, blue plate specials, and live music

Shopping
The Palafox Market
Palafox Street between Wright and Garden streets.
This open-air market with over 100 vendors is open every Saturday year-round from 9:00 a.m. to 2:00 p.m., rain or shine.

Historic Seville District Shops
Historic Seville District (South Alcaniz Street)
Pensacola, Florida 32502
Boutiques, gift shops, and art galleries

"*Even though a number
of people have tried,
no one has yet found a way
to drink for a living.*"

*- Jean Kerr (1923-2003)
U.S. author, playwright*

North Florida Wine Events and Festivals

January

Florida Wine and Grape Growers' Association Annual Meeting

Palatka, Florida

904-471-1063 – www.fgga.org

Want to learn more about growing grapes and making wine? Whether for personal consumption or to start your own commercial winery, the FWGGA annual meeting is the place to get all the information you need. Both Association members and non-members are welcome.

February

30A Wine Festival

Alys Beach, Florida

850-213-5500 – www.30awinefestival.com

Join dozens of vineyards and wineries from all over the country for a weekend of wine and food. Local restaurants present their signature dishes during this elegant, three-day fundraiser tasting event.

April

Apalachicola Art Walk and Wine Festival

Apalachicola, Florida

850-653-9419 – www.apalachicolabay.org

Fine art, a progressive wine tasting, and an evening of seafood specialties marks this art and wine festival in historic downtown Apalachicola.

Sandestin Wine Festival

Miramar Beach, Florida

www.sandestinwinefestival.com

This four-day event at Sandestin Golf and Beach Resort's Village of Baytowne Wharf is the oldest continuously running wine festival in the southeast. Activities include wine dinners, wine auctions, a wine tasting of over 800 wines, and a meet and greet of the winemakers.

South Walton Beaches Food & Wine Festival

Miramar Beach, Florida

850-837-3099 – www.sowalwine.com

Presented by Visit South Walton, this event features celebrity winemakers, distillers, chefs, and brew masters offering a four-day celebration of wine. Located at Town Center of Grand Boulevard.

May
Tangled Oaks Spring Art & Wine Festival
Grandin, Florida
386-659-1707 – www.tangledoaksvineyard.com
This celebration in the vineyard of wine, spring, and good times includes live music, craft vendors, food, wine, and free wine tastings.

Chautauqua Vineyards & Winery Spring Festival
DeFuniak Springs, Florida
850-892-5887 – www.chautauquawinery.com
Located on the winery grounds, the festival features wine tastings, tours of the winery, food, arts & crafts, and live music.

August
Old Florida Harvest Festival
Satsuma, Florida
386-467-0000 – www.logcabinfarmwinery.com
Celebrating the harvest of the grapes, Log Cabin Farm, Vineyard & Winery hosts this annual event in the vineyard with live music, food, vineyard tours, local history, and wine tastings.

September
Annual FAMU Grape Harvest Festival
Tallahassee, Florida
850-599-3413 – www.famunews.com/grape-harvest-festival
The FAMU Center for Viticulture and Small Fruit Research is the place to be for this family-friendly fun and educational festival. Activities include a grape stomping contest, a kids' petting zoo, water slides, a grape throwing competition, a grape and wine sampling, vineyard tours, and a 5K/2K vineyard run and walk-a-thon.

October
Chautauqua Vineyards & Winery Harvest Festival
DeFuniak Springs, Florida
850-892-5887 – www.chautauquawinery.com
This celebration of the harvest, located on the winery grounds features wine tastings, tours of the winery, food, arts & crafts, live music, classic cars, and a BBQ contest.

Tangled Oaks Fall Festival
Grandin, Florida
386-659-1707 – www.tangledoaksvineyard.com
This celebration in the vineyard of wine, harvest, and good times includes live music, craft vendors, food, wine, and free wine tastings.

Pensacola Beach Art & Wine Festival
Pensacola Beach, Florida
850-932-1500 – www.pensacolabeachchamber.com
Wine tasting, live music, local and regional artists, and the sound of the surf make this beachside wine event a gulf coast favorite.

Mexico Beach Art & Wine Festival
Mexico Beach, Florida
850-648-8196 – www.mexicobeach.com
Fine wines, great food, live auction, musical entertainment, and artists displaying and selling their work. The location is the Driftwood Inn.

Rosemary Beach Uncorked
Rosemary Beach, Florida
877-461-6037 – www.rosemarybeachuncorked.com
Stroll quaint cobblestone streets, taste great wine, and explore several Rosemary Beach restaurants offering their signature dishes paired with boutique wines. Proceeds benefit Habitat for Humanity.

November
Island Grove Wine Company Fall Festival and Sangria 5K Dash
Island Grove, Florida
352-481-9463 – www.islandgrovewineycompany.com
Wine tastings, winery tours, arts and crafts vendors, live music, kids' activities, and hayrides are just some of the fun. Enjoy the Outdoor Wine Lounge, or sign up for the 5k Dash through the blueberry farm. Proceeds benefit the Cross Creek Volunteer Fire Department.

Seeing Red Wine Festival
Seaside, Florida
www.seeingredwinefestival.com
This four-day wine festival at the town of Seaside includes wine tastings and winemaker dinners, with some of Seaside's restaurants showcasing their farm-to-fork and gulf-to-table cuisine paired with the featured red wines.

Wild, Wonderful Wine Recipes

Cooking with wine can be a wild and wonderful experience, mainly because wine is a wonderfully versatile cooking ingredient. Like olive oil, it's something no kitchen should be without. You can put it in soups and sauces, sauté with it, use it as a marinade or create luscious desserts. Try different wines to make different flavors in the same recipes. Just use your imagination and most of all, have fun.

A few ideas to get you started
1. Use wine in place of part of the liquid in preparing:
   - dry sauce and gravy mixes
   - cake batters, cookie doughs, puddings or pie fillings
   - homemade and condensed soups
   - stews and smothered steak
   - gelatin desserts or salads

2. After sautéing meat, pour a few tablespoons of wine into the same pan and scrape up any browned particles left from the cooking. Pour over meat and serve.

3. Add wine when reheating leftover meat, fish or poultry dishes.

4. Pour complementary wines over fresh, frozen or canned fruits.

5. For low fat cooking, sauté or stir fry vegetables in red or white wine instead of oil or butter.

6. Use dry white wine in place of water when microwaving frozen vegetables.

Wine-Baked Oysters and Crab
(*courtesy Florida Department of Agriculture*)
36 oysters in the shell
1 pound of crab meat
1/4 cup onion, finely chopped
2 tablespoons white wine or sherry
10 ounces low-fat Swiss cheese, grated

Wash oysters thoroughly. Shuck and place oysters on deep half of shell removing any remaining particles of shell. Arrange oysters on baking sheet and set aside. Combine crab meat with remaining ingredients; mix well. Top each oyster with 1 teaspoon of crab meat mixture and bake in a pre-heated oven at 450 degrees F for 10 minutes or until edges begin to curl.

Marinated Green Beans
1/4 cup dry red wine
1/3 cup lemon juice
3 tablespoons extra virgin olive oil
1/2 teaspoon celery salt
3/4 teaspoon dried dill weed
3 tablespoons finely minced onion
1/8 cup slivered almonds
1 1/2 pounds fresh or frozen green beans, cooked to taste and drained

Heat wine and lemon juice. Add oil and seasonings; pour over cooked green beans. Cover and chill thoroughly, turning occasionally to mix marinade with the beans. Serve chilled. Makes 5 to 6 servings.
(Variation: Add dark and light red kidney beans and wax beans for a bean salad. Increase the marinade ingredients depending on how many more beans you add.)

Quick Low Fat Veggie-Pasta Entree
1/2 cup yellow squash
1/2 cup zucchini
1/2 cup onion
1/2 cup red bell pepper
1/2 cup mushrooms
2 to 3 tablespoons red or white wine
2 cups cooked noodles or angel hair pasta
Fat free grated Parmesan cheese

Cut vegetables into one-inch pieces. Sauté in wine until

vegetables are tender and wine is absorbed. Spoon vegetables over cooked pasta and sprinkle with Parmesan cheese. Makes two servings.

Fried Cabbage
4 strips of bacon, diced
2 cloves crushed garlic
1 large onion, sliced
2 pounds sliced cabbage
1/2 cup chicken broth
1/2 cup dry white wine

In a large skillet or Dutch oven, sauté bacon until cooked, not crisp. Add garlic and onion. Sauté until onion is clear. Add cabbage, chicken broth and wine. Cook covered until cabbage collapses, about 5 minutes. Remove lid and cook until liquid is reduced and cabbage is tender. Do not overcook cabbage.

Stir Fry Sauce
one 15-ounce bottle of soy sauce
1 1/2 cups dry white wine
1/2 cup dry sherry
1/3 cup packed brown sugar
2 cloves garlic, cut in half
2 tablespoons chicken flavored granules
2 tablespoons grated fresh ginger root
2 teaspoons black peppercorns
1 1/2 teaspoons sesame oil

Combine all ingredients, cover and refrigerate for 8 hours. Pour through a large mesh strainer, discarding solids. Pour into bottles or jars and store in refrigerator up to 3 months. Dress up the bottles or jars for gift giving. Great for marinating chicken or pork, grilling or wok cooking. Yield 4 1/2 cups.

Wine Jelly
3 cups sugar
2 cups dry red wine
1 (3 ounce) package liquid pectin

Combine sugar and wine in a large saucepan or Dutch oven.
Cook over medium heat; stir until sugar dissolves (do not boil).
Remove from heat, stir in pectin. Skim off foam with metal
spoon. Quickly pour hot jelly into sterilized jars. Cover and
process in boiling water bath for 5 minutes. Makes 4 half pints

Wine Sauce
1 cup sugar
1/2 cup butter
1/2 cup red wine

In a large, heat resistant mixing bowl, beat butter and sugar until
light. Heat wine in saucepan until just hot. Do Not Boil. Add to
butter and sugar mixture. Place mixing bowl in a larger bowl or
pan of hot water and stir for two minutes. Serve over plum
pudding, fruit cake, or ice cream.

De Luna Dream-cicle (*courtesy De Luna Wines*)
2 oz. De Luna Strawberry Kiwi Wine
1 oz. Whipped Cream Vodka
3 oz. orange juice
Serve over ice
Whipped Cream on top

Florida Sangria
1 bottle (750 ml) of dry red wine
1 Florida orange, thinly sliced
1 lemon thinly sliced
1/2 cup sugar (optional)
1 (28 ounce) bottle Club Soda or 7-Up

Combine the wine, fruit and sugar in a large glass pitcher and let set one hour at room temperature. Just before serving, add the Club Soda or 7-Up and serve over ice. Makes 6 (8 ounce) servings

 **Muscadine Pie**
(courtesy Florida Wine & Grape Growers' Association)
4 cups Florida Muscadine Grapes
3/4 cup sugar
1 teaspoon Florida lemon juice
1 tablespoon orange rind (optional)
1/4 teaspoon ground cinnamon (optional)
pastry for 9" lattice-top pie
2 tablespoons butter or margarine, melted

Deseed grapes, reserving juice. Mix all ingredients except pie crust and butter in bowl or blender container. Let grape mixture sit for 15 minutes; pour into uncooked pie shell and top with lattice. Brush top with butter. Place pie in preheated 450-degree oven, bake for 10 minutes, then reduce heat to 350 degrees and bake for additional 20 minutes. Cool and serve plain or with whipped topping or vanilla ice cream.

Scuppernong Grape Ice
2/3 cup sugar
1 1/2 cups water
1 cup lemon juice
1/4 cup Florida orange juice
1 cup fresh Scuppernong grape juice or sparkling Scuppernong grape juice

Combine sugar and water in a heavy saucepan. Bring to a boil, stirring frequently. Boil 5 minutes. Remove from heat and add remaining ingredients, stirring well. Cool. Pour mixture into a flat tray or pan. Freeze until mixture reaches consistency of a sherbet, stirring occasionally during freezing. Scoop into sherbet dishes and serve. Makes about 1 quart

Wine Glossary

Acid, Acidity: sharp, tart effect of fruit on both the nose and tongue. Healthy grapes contain natural acidity which gives the wine its crisp, refreshing quality.

American hybrids: native grapes developed from American root stock

Aroma: perfume of fresh fruit; diminishes with fermentation and disappears with age to be replaced by the bouquet

Balanced: having all natural elements in harmony

Big: full of body and flavor; high degree of color, alcohol, and acidity

Blanc du Boise: a French-American hybrid grape developed in Florida

Body: weight and substance of wine in the mouth; actually, a degree of viscosity dependent on percentage of alcoholic and sugar content. Wines are referred to as light-bodied or full-bodied, etc.

Bouquet: fragrance that a mature wine gives off when opened; it develops further in the glass.

Brix (bricks): a scale that measures the sugar content in the juice of the grape before fermentation.

Cabernet Sauvignon: a red vinifera grape associated with the Bordeaux region in France. Often tannic when young requiring both barrel and bottle aging to soften it. Wines are complex and age well.

Cabernet Franc: similar to, and often blended with, Cabernet Sauvignon. Usually lighter in body, Cabernet Franc has a deep purple color when young and a perfumy aroma.

Carlos: a white Muscadine grape often called a Scuppernong

Catawba: a white Vitis labrusca-type grape that produces sweet white wines with a distinct foxy character. In recent years, it is also made into dry and sparkling wines.

Cayuga (ki-u-ga): A white American hybrid varietal developed in New York state that produces a light-bodied, fruity, semi-dry wine. Also called Savannah White.

Chambourcin (sham-bor-sin): a red French-American varietal that produces a soft, fruity, light-bodied, dry wine. A relative new-comer, Chambourcin has only been available commercially since 1963.

Chardonnay: a white vinifera grape that produces a dry white wine with a fruity character. It is often barrel fermented with noticeable oak flavors and aromas.

Clarity: wine should have a clear color; it should not have cloudiness or visible particles.

Clean: a well-constituted wine with no offensive smell or taste.

Concord: a red Vitis labrusca-type grape that produces a dry to semi-dry wine.

Conquistador: a hybrid, self-fertile, purple bunch grape developed at the University of Florida that is resistant to Pierce's disease and has the potential for high yield

Dry: completely lacking sugar or sweetness; not to be confused with bitterness or sourness.

Estate: 100% grapes from a winery-owned vineyard.

Fat: full-bodied but flabby. In white wines, it is often due to too much residual sugar. In red wines, it means softness and maturity.

Fermentation: the process by which yeast, combined with sugar and must, produces alcohol.

Finish: taste that wines leave in the mouth, whether pleasant or unpleasant.

Flat: dull, unattractive, low in acidity. The next stage after flabby. In sparkling wines, wine that has lost its sparkle.

Flextank: the brand name for a low cost, plastic wine tank that replicates all key barrel functions in the fermenting process.

Florida Grape Growers Association: non-profit organization established in 1923 to promote research and interest in growing grapes in Florida

Florida Farm Winery: a winery that has been issued a certificate by the Florida Department of Agriculture to be a Florida Tourist Attraction. It must produce or sell less than 250,000 gallons of wine annually, and 60% of the wine produced must be made from Florida agricultural products, maintain a minimum of 10 acres of vineyards and be open to the public for tours, tastings and sales at least 30 hours per week.

Fortified wine: a wine that has had brandy or spirits added, such as Port, Sherry or Madeira

Foxy: pronounced flavor in wines made from native American grapes usually found in young wines.

French-American hybrids: grapes that are crosses between Vitis vinifera and native American species. First developed in France in the 1800's, these grapes combine the disease resistance and winter hardiness of American species with the classic flavors of the European species.

Fruity: aroma and flavor from fresh grapes found usually in young wines.

Full bodied: a big wine with high alcoholic content and extract such as a mouth filling table wine.

Heavy: over endowed with alcohol, more than full bodied; lacking finesse.

Hybrid: grape varieties that are the product of crossing two or more Vitis species such as Vitis labrusca, Vitis rotundifolia and Vitis vinifera.

Legs: the droplets that form and ease down the sides of the glass when the wine is swirled.

Light: referring to body; low alcohol content, usually young and fruity.

Magnolia: a white Muscadine grape

Mead: wine made by fermenting honey and water, sometimes with fruits added

Medium dry: some residual sugar left. Not completely dry

Melody: a white American hybrid grape developed at Cornell University.

Merlot: a red Bordeaux-type vinifera grape that produces wines similar to Cabernet Sauvignon, with which it is often blended. These wines mature earlier than Cabernet Sauvignon and may be enjoyed as younger wines.

Muscadine: native grape found growing wild in North Carolina. White varieties are called locally by the term Scuppernong. Purple or black varieties are commonly called Muscadines.

Must: grape juice in the vat before it is converted into wine.

Niagara: a large greenish-white American hybrid with a tough skin and sweet flavor.

Nesbitt: a red Muscadine grape

Noble: a red Muscadine grape

Nose: the overall smell of wine

Oak, Oaky: a smell and taste derived from fermentation in small oak casks.

Oenology: the study of wine and winemaking

Resveratrol: an antioxidant that has been found in large quantities in Muscadine grapes and wines that is believed to be an anti-cancer agent and a possible treatment for other health conditions.

Ripe: can refer to grapes, smell and taste

Sauvignon Blanc: a white vinifera grape associated with the Bordeaux region of France. When grown in warmer climates, the flavors and aromas lean more toward spice, pear and citrus.

Scuppernong: the name given to the original variety of greeny-white or bronze colored Muscadine grapes

Seyval Blanc (say-val blonk): a white French-American varietal. Makes a dry to semi-dry, crisp, light-bodied, fruity wine. Dry versions are sometimes described as being like a French Chablis.

Soft: a mellow wine usually low in acid and tannin.

Spice: definite aroma and flavor of spice from certain grape varieties.

Suwanee: a white American hybrid grape

Sweet: having high residual sugar content, either from the grapes themselves or from added sugar or from the stopping of fermentation.

Tannin: an essential preservative extracted from the skins of red grapes during fermentation. It dries the mouth.

Unfortified: naturally fermented. Sugars can be added, but the alcohol content cannot exceed 17%.

Varietal: distinctive aroma and taste derived from a specific grape variety.

Viniculture: the cultivation of grapevines specifically for winemaking

Vintage: 95% grapes from the particular year the wine was made.

Vintner: winemaker; one who deals in wines

Viticulture: the art and science of growing grapes

Vitis labrusca: considered the American "bunch" grapes, or the American version of vinifera. Wines made from these grapes offer intense, fruity flavors.

Vitis rotundifolia: large round grapes that are native to the southeast United States are known as Muscadines. The white grape of this variety is also called Scuppernong. They are commonly eaten fresh or made into wines and jellies. Wines of this grape are rich, full-flavored, and very fruity.

Vitis vinifera: traditional European species of grapes that produce European or California-style wines.

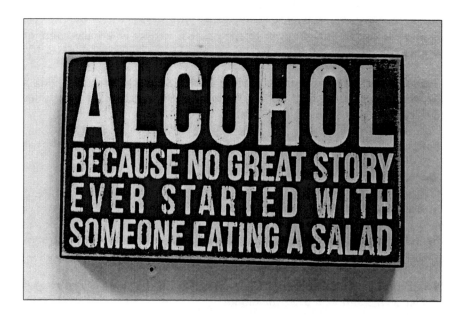

Wine Fun Facts

While you're waiting for the wine to chill...

- In computing wine production, some winemakers think in gallons and some think in cases. There are 2.38 gallons of wine in one case. Convert cases to gallons by multiplying by 2.38. Convert gallons to cases by dividing by 2.38.

- Chautauqua Vineyards & Winery is one of the state's oldest wineries. It produced its first vintage in 1989.

- The first commercial wine in America was made around 1562 by French Huguenots who settled near the St. Johns River in Florida.

- Monticello Vineyards & Winery was Florida's first organic farm winery.

- Muscadine grapes are native to the Southeastern United States.

- Muscadine vines can reach hundreds of years in age.

- In general, Muscadine red wines should be served cool but not cold.

- Florida currently has 30 Certified Farm Wineries.

- The largest single-location vineyard in Florida is Kyotee Vineyards. It has 100 acres of Muscadine grapevines.

- Florida A&M University Center for Viticulture and Small Fruit Research is located at the former Lafayette Winery in Tallahassee. It has 40 acres of vineyards and a 15,000-square foot laboratory.

- The Bible refers to the vine or wine in every book of the Old Testament except the Book of Jonah.

- California, New York, and Florida lead the United States in wine consumption.

North Florida Winery Road Trip Mileages
To create your own wine tour, here are the mileages between wineries.

San Sebastian Winery to Flagler Beachfront Winery –
    32 miles via A1A or 37 miles via I-95

San Sebastian Winery to Log Cabin Farm Vineyard and Winery –
    37 miles via State Road 207 and US 17

Flagler Beachfront Winery to Log Cabin Farm Vineyard and Winery –
    42 miles via State Road 100 and US 17

Log Cabin Farm Vineyard and Winery to Tangled Oaks Vineyard –
    32 miles via US 17 and State Road 100

Log Cabin Farm Vineyard and Winery to Royal Manor Winery –
    30 miles via US 17 and State Road 20

Tangled Oaks Vineyard and Winery to Royal Manor Winery –
    13 miles via State Road 20 and County Road 315

Tangled Oaks Vineyard and Winery to Bluefield Estate Winery –
    21 miles via CR 100, CR 26, and CR 234

Royal Manor Winery to Bluefield Estate Winery –
    27 miles via SR 20, US 301, and CR 1474

Bluefield Estate Winery to Island Grove Wine Company –
    20 miles via CR 1474, CR 26, and US 301

Bluefield Estate Winery to Micanopy Winery –
    22 miles via CR 234 and US 441

Micanopy Winery to Island Grove Wine Company Tasting House –
    18 miles via CR 325, CR 346, and US 441

Island Grove Wine Company Tasting House to Katya Vineyards or The Corkscrew Winery –
    19 miles via US 301

Micanopy Winery to Katya Vineyards or The Corkscrew Winery –
    24 miles via US 441

Micanopy Winery to Dakotah Winery –
45 miles via US 441, SR 24, Alt. US 27, and US 19

Katya Vineyards to The Corkscrew Winery –
.1 mile (two blocks)

Katya Vineyards or The Corkscrew Winery to Dakotah Winery –
56 miles via US 27 and Alt. US 27

Dakotah Winery to Mitillini Vineyards –
67 miles via US 129, CR 49, and US 90 to 76th Street

Mitillini Vineyards to Monticello Vineyards & Winery –
60 miles via I-10

Monticello Vineyards & Winery to Old Oaks Vineyard –
127 miles via I-10 and SR 79

Old Oaks Vineyard to Three Oaks Winery –
24 miles via SR 79

Three Oaks Winery to Panama City Beach Winery –
40 miles via SR 79 and US 98

Three Oaks Winery to Chautauqua Vineyards
34 miles via SR 79, CR 279 (Pate Pond Road), and I-10

Panama City Beach Winery to Emerald Coast Wine Cellars –
41 miles via US 98

Emerald Coast Wine Cellars to Chautauqua Vineyards –
37 miles via US 331 and US 98

Emerald Coast Wine Cellars to De Luna Winery
58 miles via US 98, US 90, and SR 296

Chautauqua Vineyards to De Luna Winery –
79 miles via I-10 and I-110

De Luna Winery to San Sebastian Winery –
393 miles via I-10 and I-95 ☺

Useful Contacts

Visit Florida
850-488-560, 866-972-5280 – www.visitflorida.com
VISIT FLORIDA is the official tourism marketing corporation for the State of Florida. Go online or call to order an Official Florida Vacation Guide and other planning materials or to speak to a VISIT FLORIDA representative about Florida tourism.

Florida Wine and Grape Growers' Association
P.O. Box 840256, St. Augustine, Florida 32080
904-471-1063 – www.fgga.org
The Florida Grape Growers' Association is committed to developing a locally organized and sustainable agricultural community in Florida. Members include winery owners and managers, hobbyists, viticulture science professionals and others interested in growing grapes and making wine. Membership includes a newsletter, savings at participating wineries and other grape products locations, reduced admission to the annual conference, leadership opportunities as a board or committee member and networking opportunities with viticulture experts and hobbyists.

Florida Department of Agriculture
Division of Marketing and Development
The Mayo Building
407 South Calhoun Street, Tallahassee, Florida 32399
850-617-7314 – www.freshfromflorida.com/wine
The Florida Department of Agriculture oversees licensing and regulation in the grape and wine industry. See their web site for a list of certified Florida wineries, for brochures or for information about Florida Farm Winery licensing.

Try Florida Wine
www.tryfloridawine.com
Sponsored by the FWGGA, this website features Florida wineries, wine history, and wine and health articles.

Southern Wine Trails
www.southernwinetrails.net
Find wineries and more on my blog about wine in the South

Index

Find More Florida Wine
Central & South Florida Wineries

Aspirations Winery, *Clearwater* 727-799-9463

Bunker Hill Vineyard and Winery, *Duette* 941-776-0418

Empire Winery and Distillery, *New Port Richey* 727-819-2821

Florida Estates Winery, *Land O' Lakes* 813-996-2113

Florida Orange Groves Inc. and Winery, *St. Petersburg* 1-800-338-7923

Grapes of Kath Vineyards, *Sebring* 863-382-4706

Henscratch Farms Vineyard and Winery, *Lake Placid* 863-699-2060

Hutchinson Farm Winery, *Apopka* 407-814-8330

Keel and Curley Winery, *Plant City* 813-752-9100

Lakeridge Winery and Vineyards, *Clermont* 1-800-768-9463

Masaryk Winery, *Masaryktown* 352-308-0110

Murielle Winery, *Clearwater* 727-561-0336

Oak Haven Farms and Winery, *Sorrento* 352-735-1996

Rosa Fiorelli Winery Inc., *Bradenton* 941-322-0976

Schnebly Redland's Winery and Brewery, *Homestead* 305-242-1224

Sons and Daughters Farm and Winery, *Lake Worth* 305-613-8039

Strong Tower Vineyard and Winery, *Spring Hill* 352-799-7612

Sparacia-Witherell Family Winery and Vineyards, *Brooksville*
919-366-2509

Summer Crush Vineyard and Winery, *Fort Pierce* 772-460-0500

Tarpon Springs Castle Winery, *Tarpon Springs* 727-943-7029

Time to Make Wine Inc., *Fort Myers* 239-542-9463

The Florida Winery, *Madeira Beach* 727-362-0008

True Blue Winery, *Davenport* 863-419-4400

Whispering Oaks Winery, *Oxford* 352-748-0449